Our Eyes Are On God

5 Minute Sunday Morning Devotions

Rebecca Lutman Collins

ISBN: Number

Columbus Book Publishers
www.columbusbookpublishers.com

Printed in the United States of America

Dedication

I want to dedicate this book to my parents, Ray and Marie Lutman, who raised me in a Christian home. They made it their priority to gift me with the opportunity to know Jesus and find Salvation at a young age.

I also want to thank my friends who encouraged me to write a devotional.

About the Book

Our Eyes Are On God is a series of five minute devotions for Sunday mornings that are easy to read before going to worship. When reading these devotions, use them to be close to God's Word with reflection as you prepare to go to your worship service on the Lord's Day. Reading God's word through a devotional on Sunday morning is an inspirational way to begin your journey to your place of worship. These devotions help you to reflect on the Bible and encounter spiritual topics and encourage you to also spend time in prayer before going to worship. These devotions have their place making Scripture more approachable, helping you to apply what you read to your life and prepare your heart for worship.

Jesus reinforces this idea of devotions when he reminds us that our Father knows what we need and will give it to us. Revealing the fundamental purpose of personal devotions, Jesus said in Mathew 6:33 *"But seek first the kingdom of God and his righteousness, and all these things will be done."* The primary focus of a devotional is to encourage reflection, prayer and a deeper connection with our faith. These devotions are a great way to start the Lord's Day by spending time with God and preparing your heart for worship. When we attend worship regularly, we become better worshippers. It helps us to focus more on God and less on ourselves. When we attend services, we receive spiritual nourishment from the Lord which strengthens us spiritually and helps us grow in our faith. Worship is a declaration that God is in the midst and in control of all that is happening in our world today. Here are just five reasons to spend devotional time on Sunday mornings before worship.

1.   It reminds us of what we already have.
2.   It softens our hearts towards God.
3.   It softens our hearts towards others.
4.   It prepares our hearts for worship.
5.   It opens up our desire to share the truth of the Gospel.

Devotions are like exercises for our souls. They pull our attention off of self-indulgent distractions and pursuits and on to God's promises and purposes. If we neglect this exercise our souls will suffer. These devotions help to create an intimate space between you and God, allowing Him to speak directly to your heart in such a way that you are drawn nearer to Him. As a result, He is glorified, and you go deeper into identity with Him. Sunday morning's devotions are a heart connection. They reach into places of encouragement, inspiration, motivation, enthusiasm, love and leading to worship. Sunday morning devotions is a spiritual discipline that helps us get to know God and ensures us that we stay connected to Him. It teaches us truth that provides us a place for worship and provides us a shelter in the midst of the storms of life. Building a close relationship with God requires "heart" work, slowing down to take time for a devotional and trusting God instead of ourselves. I hope, when you sit in a quiet place with this devotional book, that you converse with God and prepare your heart for a glorious worship service filled with blessings.

Table of Contents

Psalm 139

"O Lord, you have searched me, and you know me. You know, when I sit, and when I rise, you perceive my thoughts from afar. You discern my going out and my lying down; you are familiar with all of my ways. Before a word is on my tongue, you know it completely, 0 Lord. You hem me in - behind and before; you have laid your hand upon me. Such knowledge is too wonderful for me, too lofty for me to attain. Where can I go from your Spirit? Where can I flee from your presence? If I go up to the heavens, you are there; if I make my bed in the depths, you are there. If I rise on the wings of the dawn, if I settle on the far side of the sea. Even there, your hand will guide me; your right hand will hold me fast. If I say, 'Surely the darkness will hide me and the light become night around me,' Even the darkness will not be dark to you; the night will shine like the day, for darkness is as light to you. For you created my inmost being; you knit me together in my mother's womb.

I praise you because I am fearfully and wonderfully made; your works are wonderful; I know that full well. My frame was not hidden from you when I was made in the secret place. When I was woven together in the depths of the earth, your eyes saw my unformed body. All the days ordained for me were written in your book before one of them came to be. How precious concerning me are your thoughts, O God! How vast is the sum of them. Were I to count them, they would outnumber the grains of sand. When I awake I am still with you... Search me, O God, and know my heart; test me and know my anxious thoughts. See if there is any offensive way in me, and lead me in the way everlasting."

Faith

As I prepare for worship this morning, I am thinking about faith and how it has carried me through some hard times. Having faith in Jesus Christ means relying completely on Him, trusting in His infinite power and love. It includes believing in His teachings. It means believing that even though we do not understand all things, He does because He has experienced our pains. Faith is a decision to believe; it is a choice, not a feeling. Faith does not make things easy… it makes things possible!

In Hebrews, there is a verse that is often quoted and is considered the Bible's closest definition of faith. Hebrews 11:1 defines faith as "the assurance of things hoped for, the conviction of things not seen."

"For by grace you have been saved through faith. And this is not your own doing; it is the gift of God." **Ephesians 2:8**

Wherever you worship today, May your heart be filled with faith and joy.

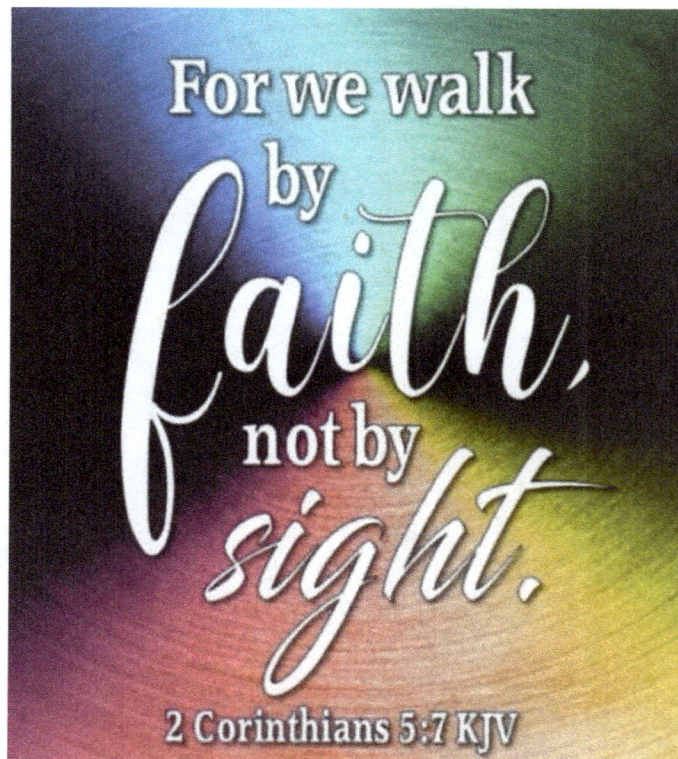

For we walk by faith, not by sight.
2 Corinthians 5:7 KJV

Using Our Gift

As I prepare for worship this morning, gifts come to my mind. The gifts I am talking about are the gifts God has given to each one of us to use for His glory. There are so many gifts: teaching, caring, encouraging, praying, and kindness—these are just a few. Some people have gifts that seem to outshine others, but in God's eyes, every gift He has given us is of equal importance in His plan. It is our choice to choose to use the gift He has given to us for His glory. Satan fools some into thinking they do not have anything to offer, and Satan takes great joy in that. If you are not yet using your gift or have not found it yet, please pray about it, and God will reveal it to you. Remember that your gift, no matter if you think it is too small, is of great importance to God and His plan for you.

"But each of you has your own gift from God; one has this gift, another has that." **1 Corinthians 7:7 NIV**

"Each of you should use whatever gift you have received to serve others, as faithful stewards of God's grace in its various forms." **1 Peter 4:10**

Wishing you a day of worship filled with joy, praise, and blessings.

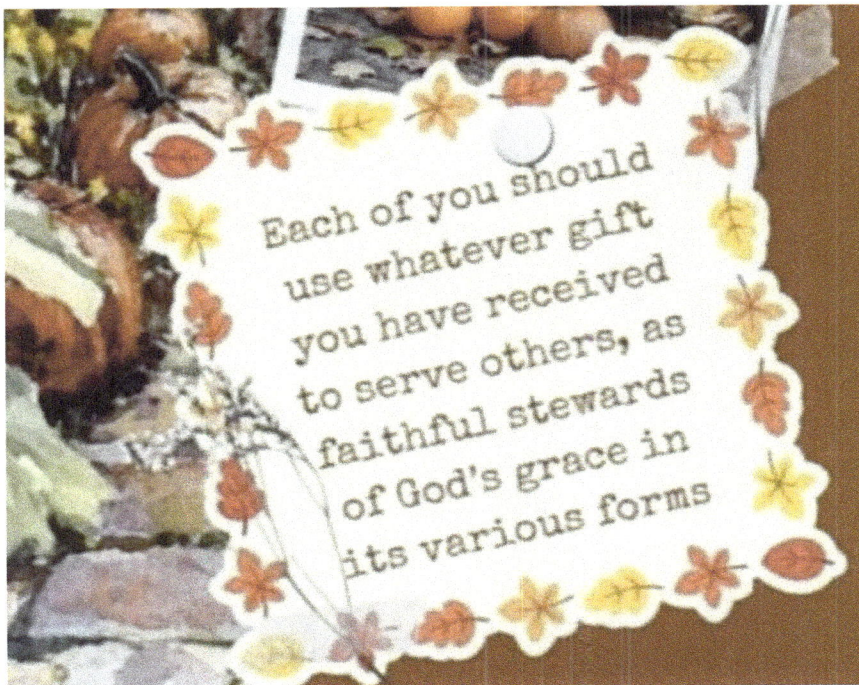

Each of you should use whatever gift you have received to serve others, as faithful stewards of God's grace in its various forms

Spiritual Winter

As I prepare for worship on this cold winter day, I am thinking about all the ice and snow we have had. I have heard stories of how dangerous the roads were. But this made me think of the dangers of "spiritual winters" and how they are even more dangerous. They can destroy families, chill churches, and darken our hearts.

We can stay indoors, pop on an extra layer, or snuggle under a blanket when we're chilly in the winter. But most importantly, we must keep our hearts and souls warm by reading God's word and spending time in prayer so that we do not experience a "spiritual winter." The more you know God from reading the Bible, the more you desire him and are changed for the better. You experience more peace and live a better life.

"But Jesus answered, "It is written: 'Man shall not live on bread alone, but on every word that comes from the mouth of God." **Matthew 4:4**

Wishing you a glorious day of worship filled with many blessings.

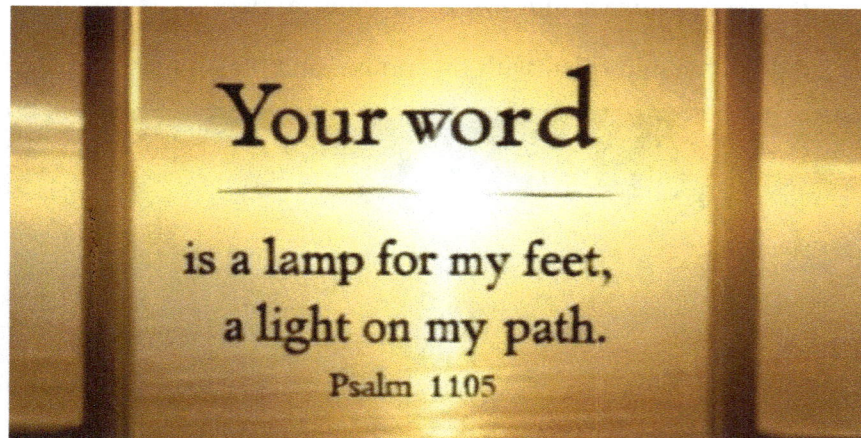

Your word is a lamp for my feet, a light on my path. Psalm 1105

Inheritance

The older I get, the faster Sundays seem to come around. I am grateful that God has granted me another Sabbath in which to praise and worship him. Recently, I heard a friend talking about the inheritance she received when her mother passed away. An inheritance is promised when someone is alive but granted when they die. Usually, inheritances pass from a parent to a child or children.

I know that I am a child of God, and I have the greatest of all inheritances waiting for me in Heaven because Jesus is my Savior. This inheritance is greater than any wealth, material things, or anything found here on earth. A believer's inheritance is not of this world but rather a glorious possession that will never diminish and is unfading and enduring. Our inheritance is eternity in Heaven with the Lord.

Ephesians teaches us this, the believer's inheritance is two-fold. First, it means becoming a child of God; this gives us the right to expect an inheritance. Second, we gain eternity with the Lord, dwelling in His righteousness for all time.

"Yet to all who did receive him, to those who believe in his name, he gave the right to become children of God."
John 1:12

Have you received Jesus as your Savior? Are you a child of God? Do you have an inheritance waiting for you in Heaven?

I wish each of you a day of worship filled with praise, joy, and thankfulness.

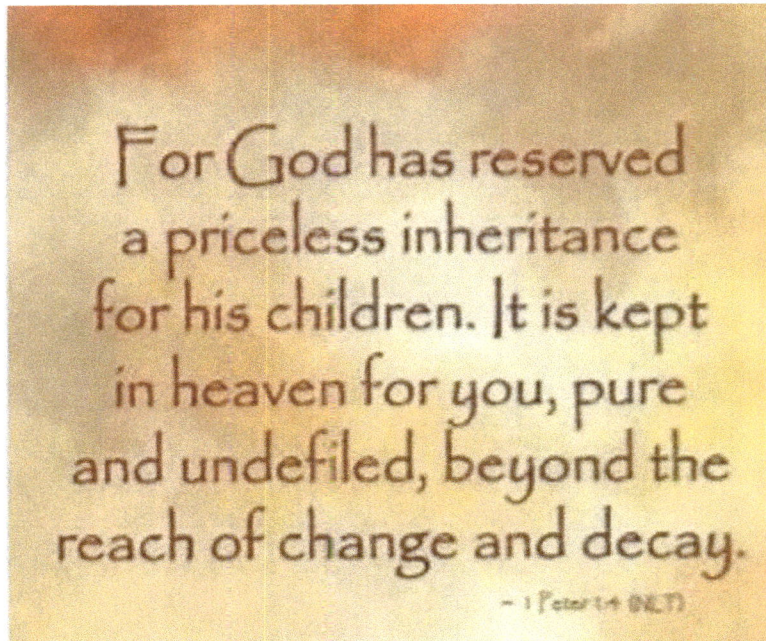

For God has reserved a priceless inheritance for his children. It is kept in heaven for you, pure and undefiled, beyond the reach of change and decay.
— 1 Peter 1:4 (NLT)

The Narrow Path

As I prepare for worship today, I am thinking about the narrow path that my Bill shoveled to the mailbox the other day. That path brought these words from scripture to mind...

"Enter through the narrow gate. For wide is the gate, and broad is the road that leads to destruction, and many enter through it. But small is the gate, and narrow is the road that leads to life, and only a few find it." **Matthew 7:13-14**

As I looked at Bill's pathway, its narrowness made me think of how easy it would be to step off of it. But, if I did, I would slip into the snow and fall. The better I know God, the more I am able to trust Him in the dark times, the more willing I am to accept His Word as direction for my life, and the more likely I will be to walk the path He has for me. The narrow path is not easy to follow, but following the narrow path will lead to a meaningful and fulfilling life, both in this world and in eternity.

As you worship today, I wish you the joy of walking and talking with our Lord. Have a beautiful day filled with blessings.

Second Chances

As I prepare for worship on this Lord's Day, I am thinking about second chances and how many times God has granted them to me, knowing that I am so far from perfect. Second chances embody grace and renewal. God gave Moses a second chance to return to Egypt and free the Israelites. God gave Jonah a second chance to preach after Jonah fled from God's calling.

There is also Peter and David. God giving people second chances is based on the belief that God is patient and forgiving. The Bible says that God gives me multiple chances to fulfill my purpose in life, and for that, I am eternally grateful!

If you are thinking you do not deserve a second chance from God, it is important to remember that you did not deserve the first one either.

"If we confess our sins, he is faithful and just to forgive us our sins and to cleanse us from all unrighteousness." ***1 John 1:9***

I wish you a day of worship filled with praise, joy, and blessings.

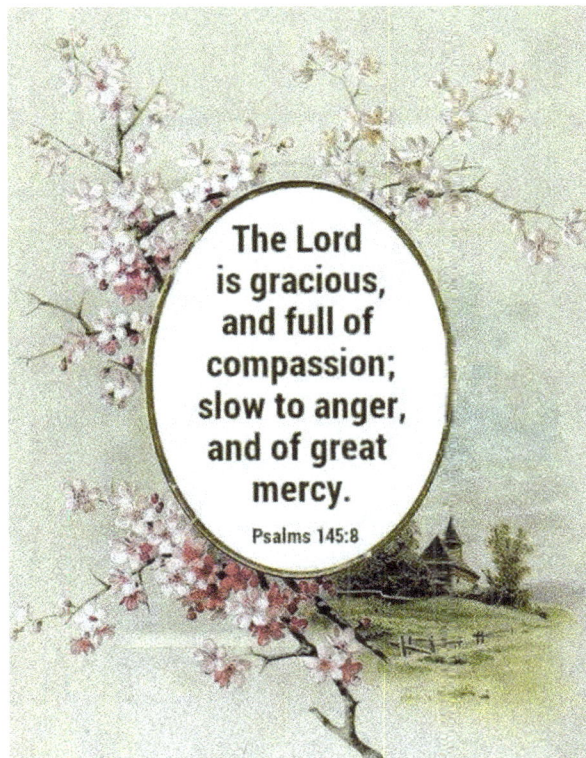

The Lord
is gracious,
and full of
compassion;
slow to anger,
and of great
mercy.

Psalms 145:8

Crossing a Bridge

As I prepare for worship this morning, I am reminded of a photo of a footbridge that I saw this week. Many times, God has asked me to cross a bridge like that, and it was sometimes a hard choice for me. I would wonder if I should even take that first step or maybe turn around halfway and come back. But, by crossing that bridge, I learned to put my trust in God and strengthened my faith.

Trust acts like a bridge that helps us move forward in faith. When we lean on God's wisdom rather than our own, He guides us on the right path, strengthening our bond with Him. Are you willing to cross that bridge when God calls you?

"Trust in the Lord with all your heart; do not depend on your own understanding. Seek his will in all you do, and he will show you which path to take." **Proverbs 3:5-6**

Wishing you a day of worship seeking God's will for you and filled with joy and blessings.

Share the Good News

As I prepare for worship this morning, I would like to share the Good News with you. As a believer, I know these things to be true: The Bible is the word of god. Jesus is the only Savior sent by god. The Gospel is the power of God. Life is for the glory of God. In these things, I have the courage, faith, and confidence to share the good news that Jesus has won the victory for you and me.

> *"And this is the testimony: God has given us eternal life, and this life is in his Son. Whoever has the Son has life; whoever does not have the Son of God does not have life."*
> **1 John 5:11-12**

I am forever grateful for the Cross, the Tomb, and the Resurrection. Who will you share the Good News with?

Wishing you a glorious day of worship.

"Jesus said, 'Go and tell the good news.'" Mark 16:15

Idols

As I prepare for worship today, my scripture reading is talking about idols. An idol is anything that becomes more important in our life than God. The Old Testament of the Bible talks a lot about God's sadness with his people worshipping idols, which are false gods. Today, our idols may be things like money, career, possessions, and status. Even family can become our idol.

Everyone who idolizes these kinds of things will never find satisfaction in them. It seems to me that phones, iPads and computers have become idols for some. In modern times, idolatry can include putting trust in things other than God.

When we put something else in the place of God, we are in danger of losing spiritual hearing and spiritual seeing. We lose the ability to walk in God's ways and see that the Lord is good. Putting anything in the place of God will shrink your soul.

> *"Formerly, when you did not know God, you were slaves to those who, by nature, are not gods. But now that you know God, or rather are known by God, how is it that you are turning back to those weak and miserable forces? Do you wish to be enslaved by them all over again?"* **Galatians 4:8-9**

Wishing you a glorious day of worship that fills your heart with joy.

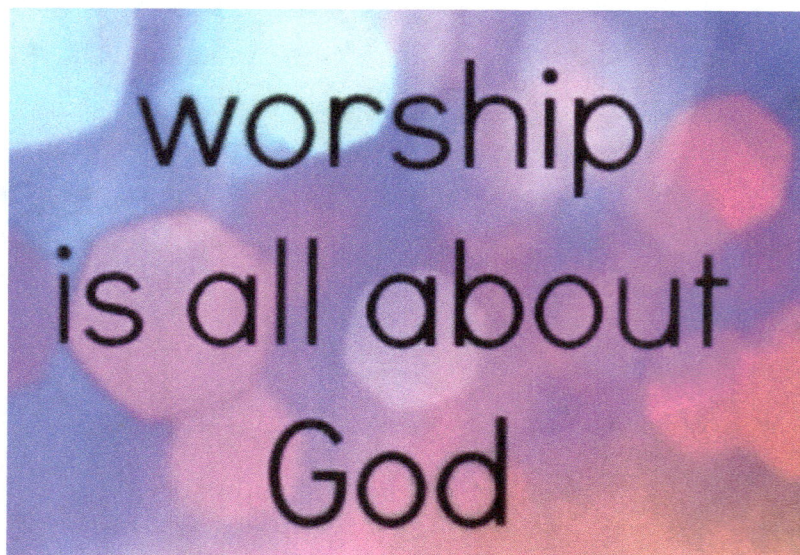

worship is all about God

Is Your Boat Sinking?

As I am preparing for worship today, I am thinking about a saying I read the other day. It said a boat does not sink because it is in the water. It sinks because the water gets into it. There have been times when I have found myself in a sinking boat by my own doing.

It made me think that I do not sin and fall short because I am in the world but because I let the world in me. I find that I need to plug the holes with the truth of God's Word by reading the Scriptures.

Is your boat sinking? Is it being swamped by the world? In many ways, the boat served as a symbol of our faith. Do not let your boat get shipwrecked by worldly ideas.

"Do not be conformed to this age, but be transformed by the renewing of your mind, so that you may discern what is the good, pleasing, and perfect will of God." **Romans 12:2**

Wishing you a beautiful day of worship filled with faith, praise, and blessings.

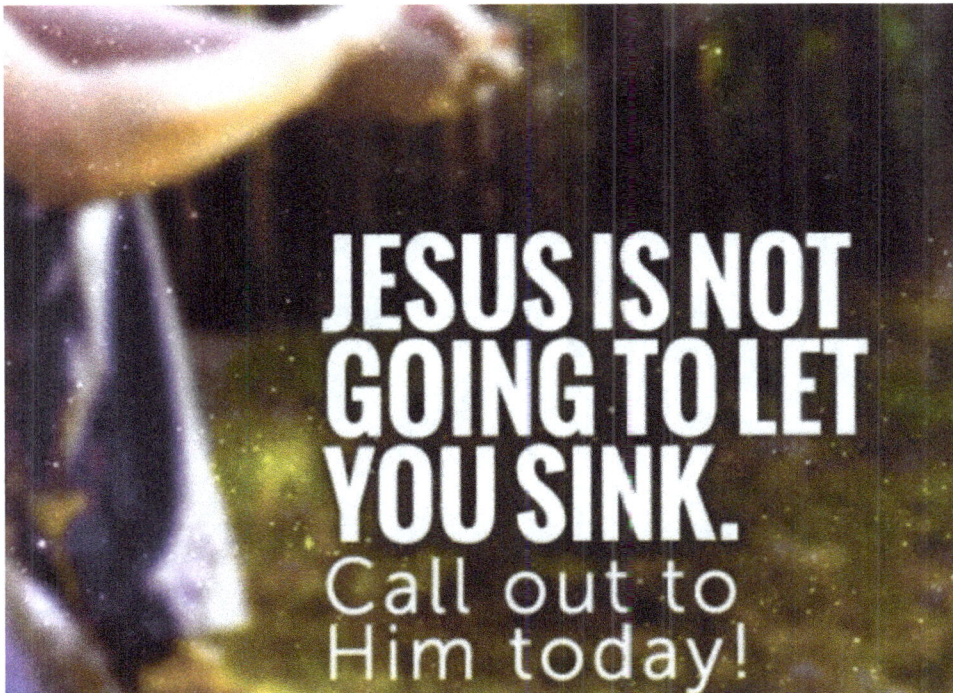

JESUS IS NOT GOING TO LET YOU SINK. Call out to Him today!

Missions

As I sit here in my cozy recliner and prepare for worship today, missions are on my mind. All the way through the Bible, from Genesis to Revelations, God tells us how serious He is about missions. God desires for the whole world to know about him. We can support missions in three ways: by praying, giving and going. There are missionaries all over the world doing God's work. But there are also missionaries right here at home. Missions are inseparable from our faith. Proclaiming the Gospel isn't just important because we are commanded to do it. God uses us to bring the good news of Jesus to those who need our Savior. It comes hand in hand with our faith in Christ.

> *"Therefore go and make disciples of all nations, baptizing them in the name of the Father and of the Son and the Holy Spirit, and teaching them to obey everything I have commanded you. And surely I am with you always, to the very end of age."* **Mathew 28:19-20**

We need to always be in prayer for missionaries that God may keep them safe and healthy and open doors for them as they do His work.

Wishing you a glorious day of worship filled with many blessings.

MISSIONS
LOCAL · STATEWIDE · WORLDWIDE

I Stand Amazed

I have been blessed with yet another glorious Lord's Day. There is a hymn I love to sing, and it is "I Stand Amazed." Charles Gabriel wrote this hymn, but the background of this particular hymn is not known. It is an incredible expression of joy at God's goodness and grace. I find myself humming the chorus this morning...

How marvelous! How wonderful! And my song shall ever be. How marvelous! How wonderful is my Savior's love for me!

"The Lord your God is in your midst, a mighty one who will save you. He will rejoice over you with gladness." **Zephaniah 3:17**

I hope you know this hymn. If not, take a few minutes and look it up, and it will bless you. Wishing you joy as you worship on this day that God has granted you.

Happiness

As I prepare for worship on this Lord's Day, I am thinking about happiness. We all want to be happy, but sometimes, it can be a struggle because we search for it in all the wrong places or ways of life. Satan tempts us with what looks like happiness in many worldly things, but as Christians, we soon find out those things do not bring us any happiness. Satan takes great joy when he has that kind of victory over us.

This is how we can ask God for happiness...

Lord, please send me peace through your Holy Spirit. I want to be happy and peaceful in the life You have given me and in all the circumstances of life. Your Spirit brings peace and happiness, and I ask for that, in the name of Jesus Christ, Amen.

"Happy are the people whose strength is in You, whose hearts are set on pilgrimage. God is our strength, and our happiness is found there, in Him." **Psalm 84:5**

Wishing everybody a day of worship filled with praise and happiness.

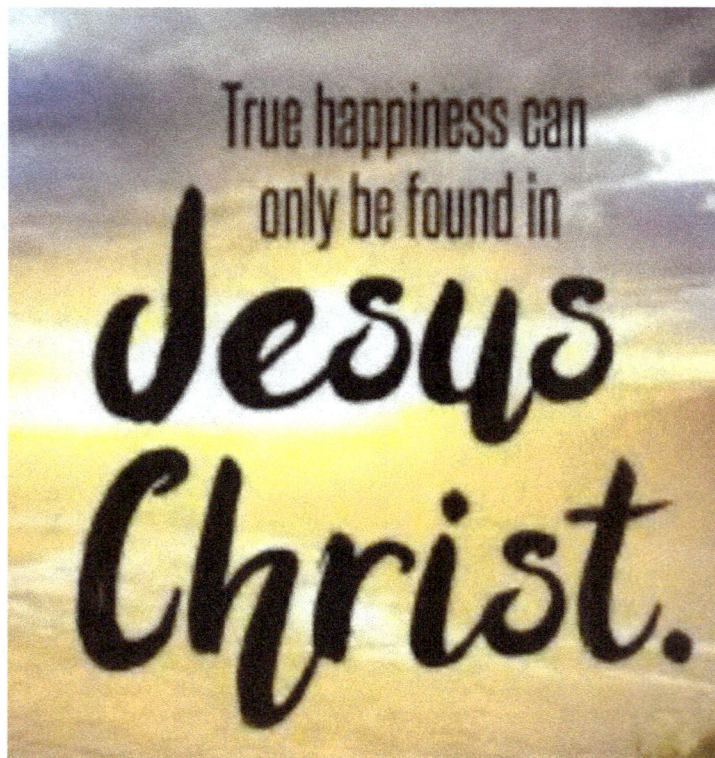

True happiness can only be found in Jesus Christ.

Living Water

I woke up to another Lord's Day, and I am grateful for it. With Autumn too soon to be upon us, I peeked outside to see the remaining blooms on the flowers, and the lawns were still green. God has blessed us with just enough rain this summer so we can enjoy the beauty of Summer's bounty. But, very soon, the flowers and gardens will turn to seed. This made me think of my own soul. As long as I keep it watered with Scripture, worship, and prayer time, Jesus will fill my soul with His beauty through each season of my life. If I find myself too busy for Jesus, my soul can turn brown and empty like a summer with too much heat and little rain. In many ways, our souls are like gardens that need regular watering to stay healthy. Spiritual watering involves reading the Bible, prayer, and worshipping.

"As the deer pants for streams of water, so my soul pants for you, my God." **Psalm 42:1**

"O God, you are my God, earnestly I seek you; my soul thirsts for you." **Psalm 63:1**

Wishing you a day of worship that waters your soul and fills you with joy.

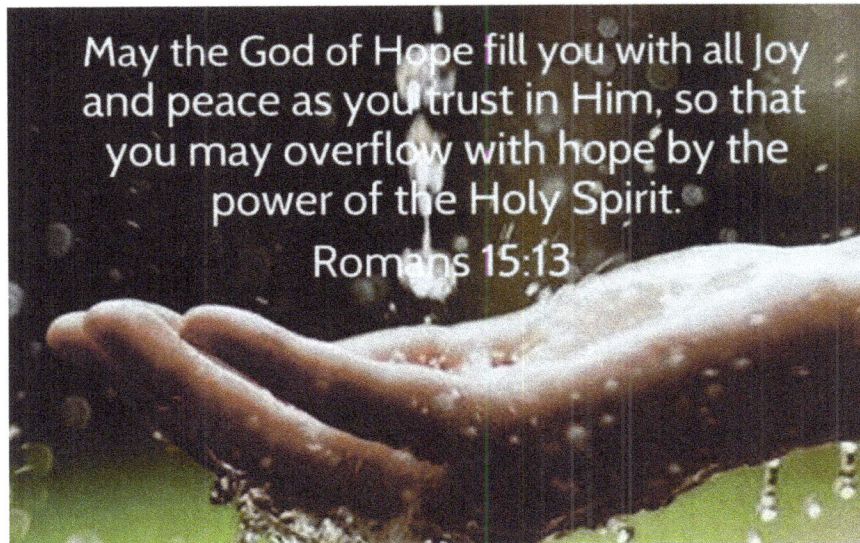

May the God of Hope fill you with all Joy and peace as you trust in Him, so that you may overflow with hope by the power of the Holy Spirit.
Romans 15:13

Following God's Path

God has granted me yet another Lord's Day to worship. I recently heard the words "pondering" and "stumbling," and I find that I do both. There are times I find myself "stumbling" spiritually because I am "pondering" about things of no consequence instead of God's word. But, by His grace, God invites me to place my steps with care through his words.

Following God's path is a dedicated commitment to live according to God's will. It is actively seeking guidance through prayer and studying scripture. It's about surrendering our own desires to God's plan and allowing Him to lead the way.

"The Lord makes firm the steps of the one who delights in Him; though he may stumble, he will not fall, for the Lord upholds him with His hand." **Psalms 27:23-24**

"Make a level path for your feet, and all your ways will be sure. Give careful thought to the paths for your feet and be steadfast in all your ways." **Proverbs 4:26**

Wishing you a day of worship filled with blessings and a path guided by God.

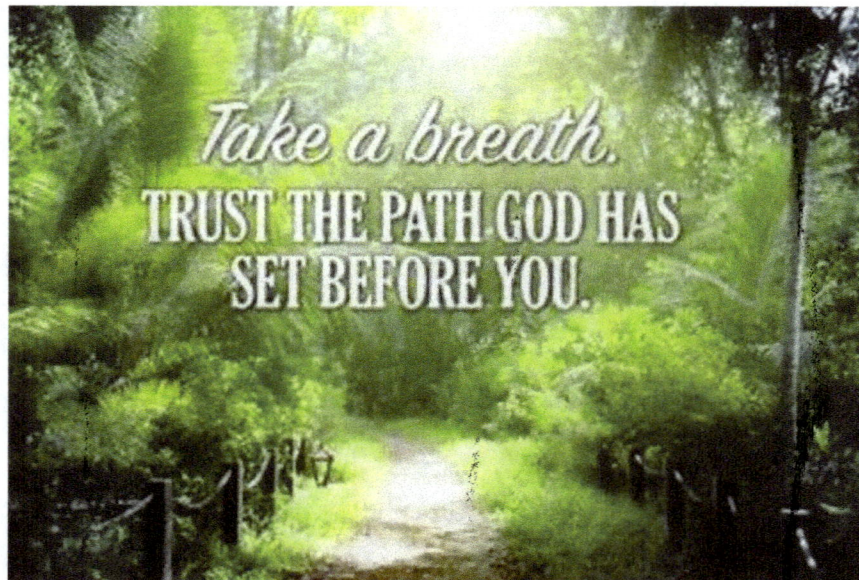

God's Way

As I prepare for worship this morning, I want to share with you one of the most valuable lessons I have learned in my lifetime, and that, in everything I do, I have two choices.

Choice number one: Will I do it my way?

Choice number two: Will I do it God's way?

The Bible says that God's way is perfect, refreshing, trustworthy, and right. I don't know about you, but my way usually isn't any of those things. Amazingly, God's way is not only all those things, but it also meets me wherever I am. Living my life in God's way has always proven to be rewarding to me.

"In all your ways submit to him, and he will make your paths straight." **Proverbs 3:6**

"Teach me your way, ah Lord; I will walk in your truth; unite my heart to fear your name." **Psalms 86:11**

Wishing you a day of worship that fills your heart with joy.

Show me Your ways, O LORD; Teach me Your paths. PSALM 25:4

God is My Refuge

As I prepare for worship this morning, my mind is on Israel, Ukraine, and the troubles around the world as well as in our own country. I pray these wars do not come to our doorsteps. I know I need to humble myself in prayer, turn to God, open His word, and trust what He says. I know I need to adjust my heart to His truth, not allowing the world's appearance to steer me. I know I need to lean not on my own understanding or self-doubting but on God's specific words and promises to me in the Bible.

"Trust in the LORD with all thine heart, and lean not unto thine own understanding."
Proverbs 3:5

"Do not gloat over me, my enemy. Though I have fallen, I will rise. Though I sit in darkness, the LORD will be my light." **Micah 7:8**

Please be in prayer with me for those who are so desperately trying to escape war and persecution around the world.

Wishing you a day of worship filled with blessings and brings peace to your heart.

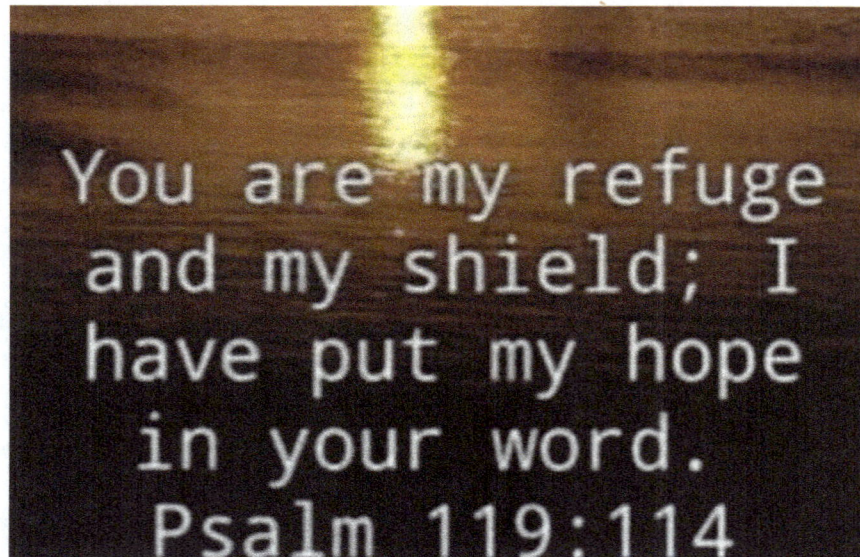

You are my refuge and my shield; I have put my hope in your word. Psalm 119:114

Thankful for Blessings

As I am preparing for worship on this Lord's Day, I find myself thinking of so many blessings God has given me that I take for granted and how I need to be more thankful. I have so much that so many can only dream about having. I am talking about the basics of life and how easy it is to become complacent about these blessings. All that I have has been given to me by God, even the air I breathe, and yet, there are times I fail to thank Him for blessing me with so much that others struggle without.

Thankfulness not only praises God in the moment but also remembers God's past faithfulness. It is a statement of God's character, which is so wonderful that praise and thankfulness through prayer is the only appropriate response.

This scripture is speaking to my heart this morning.

"Give thanks in all circumstances, for this is God's will for you in Christ Jesus." **1 Thessalonians 5:18**

Wishing you a day of worship filled with thankfulness for what you have been blessed with.

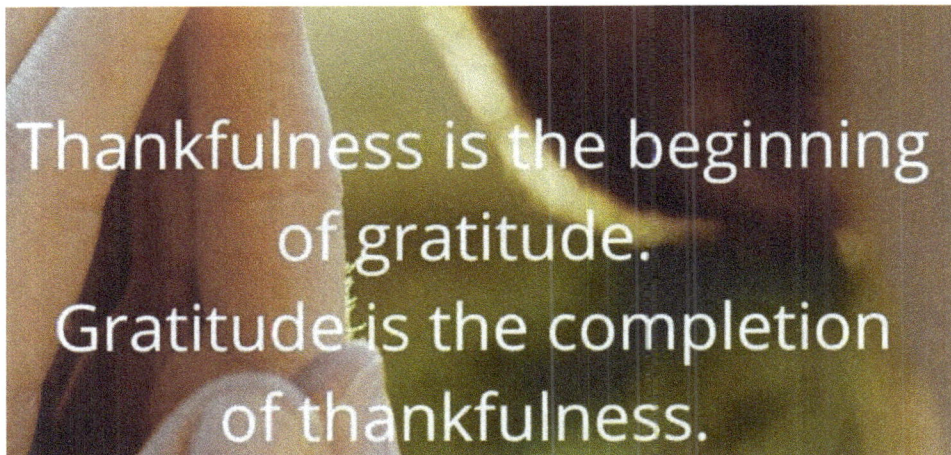

Thankfulness is the beginning of gratitude. Gratitude is the completion of thankfulness.

His Eye is on the Sparrow

What a beautiful day God has given us on this Lord's Day, and I find myself humming the song "His Eye Is On The Sparrow." I find happiness in doing the will of God. The purest joy comes from knowing Jesus. Happiness is found in the beauty and wonders of Jesus. I express my happiness in worshipping my Savior.

I SING BECAUSE I'M HAPPY; I SING BECAUSE I'M FREE. HIS EYE IS ON THE SPARROW, AND I KNOW HE WATCHES ME. ME.

"Fear ye not therefore, ye are of more value than many sparrows..." **Matthew 10:31**

The Lord will watch over your coming and going both now and forevermore. **Psalm 121:8**

I wish you happiness on this Lord's Day and a day of worship filled with blessings.

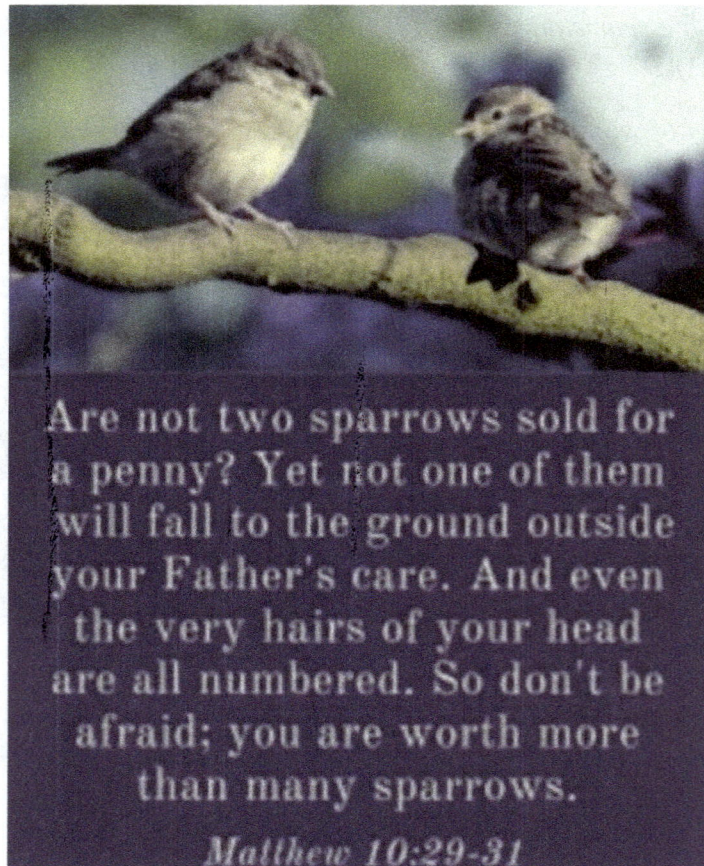

Are not two sparrows sold for a penny? Yet not one of them will fall to the ground outside your Father's care. And even the very hairs of your head are all numbered. So don't be afraid; you are worth more than many sparrows.

Matthew 10:29-31

Freedom

God has granted me another Lord's Day, and I am grateful. Most years, by September in Missouri, everything has started to turn brown, and most flowers and gardens are going to seed from lack of rain. This makes me think of my soul and how I must keep it watered with Scripture, worship, and prayer time. But, if I find myself too busy for Jesus, my soul becomes empty and brown like a September that has had too much heat and little rain.

We are so blessed in this country to be able to fill our souls with Jesus all the time, any time, and wherever we choose. There may come a time when we could lose this freedom. I never really thought that could happen until 9/11/2001. That was the first time I actually realized I could lose my freedom to openly worship. Don't let this freedom become lost to you because worshipping is a command from our God, and we do it out of great love and thankfulness for Him. I hope we all show our Savior our gratitude for our freedom of all kinds, especially the freedom to worship.

"Now the Lord is the Spirit, and where the Spirit of the Lord is, there is freedom." **2 Corinthians 3:17**

Wishing each of you a glorious day of worship filled with God's blessings.

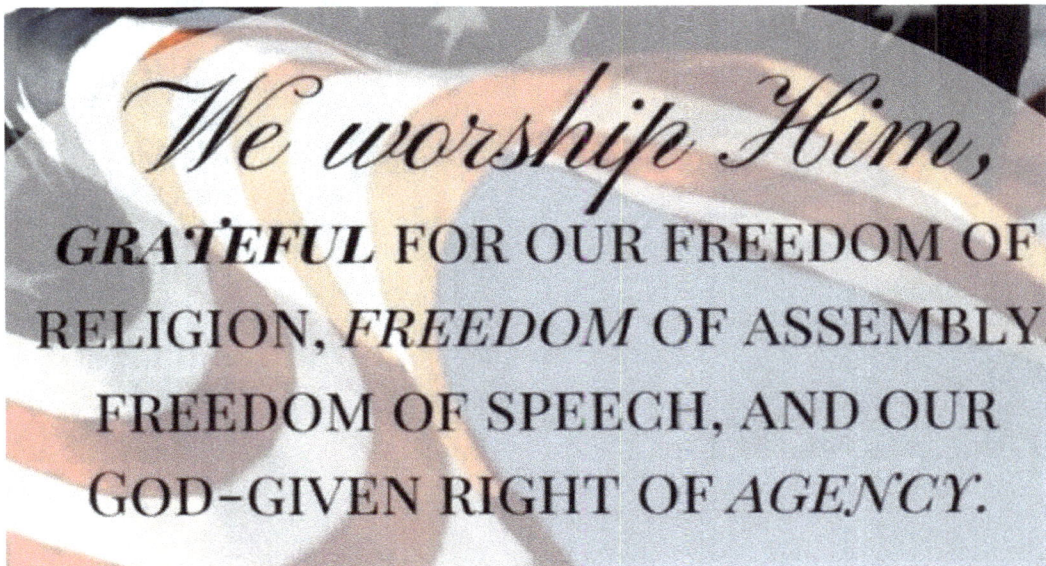

We worship Him, GRATEFUL FOR OUR FREEDOM OF RELIGION, *FREEDOM* OF ASSEMBLY, FREEDOM OF SPEECH, AND OUR GOD-GIVEN RIGHT OF *AGENCY.*

Time

Here I am, blessed with another Lord's Day. Time is on my mind today since it is the day we set our clocks back an hour. There were times when I wished I could turn the clock back and have a redo… when I could just change a word or action that could have made a difference in my life or someone else.

God's Word advises us to use our time wisely because He knows that there are many things in life that can distract us from what truly matters. Do not waste your time so that you look back with regret - you do not know what tomorrow holds! Making time for worship, reading God's word, spending time alone with God, and praying are gifts of time that are not to be wasted.

"Yet you do not know what tomorrow will bring. What is your life? For you are a mist 1hat appears for a little time and then vanishes." **James 4:14**

"Look carefully at how you walk, not as unwise but as wise, making the best use of the time because the days are evil." **Ephesians 5:15-16**

I wish you time to worship our Lord and a day filled with blessings.

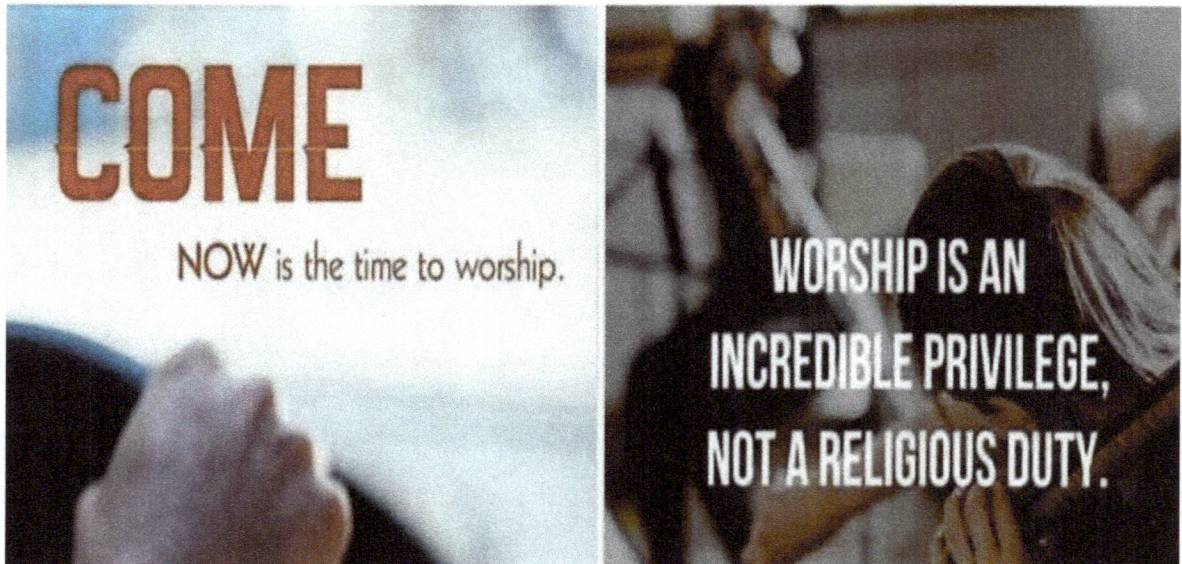

The Gift of Prayer

As I prepare for worship this morning, my mind is on the most amazing gift of prayer. It is so powerful, and we can pray anywhere, at any place, and at any time. We do not need eloquent words because God knows our hearts and hears our words, even if they are simple. God's answers are not always what we want, but He always knows what is best for us and the plan He has for our lives.

"Be careful for nothing, but in everything by prayer and supplication with thanksgiving, let your requests be made known unto God. And the peace of God, which passed all understanding, shall keep your hearts and minds through Christ Jesus." **Philippians 4:6-7**

I find it of great importance to lift up our loved ones and our friends when they are in need or struggling with a battle. I am grateful for all the answered prayers in my life and for the people who have prayed for me. Don't waste this gift, and be a prayer warrior.

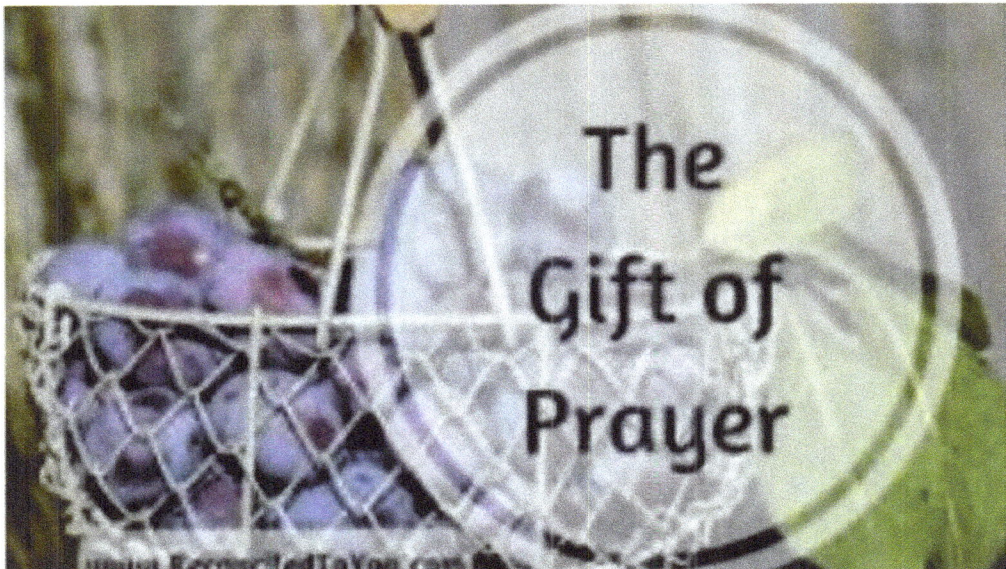

The Gift of Autumn

Getting ready for worship this morning, I peeked out my window to look at the trees and the beautiful colors that are now surrounding my home. Every year, the changing colors of Fall amaze me. As a child, I remember taking long rides to see all the trees in their magnificent colors. It is a tradition I have kept up all my life. When I was little, I thought God painted the trees at night just for us. For many years now, I have understood that they are, in fact, God's creation, and this season is a gift from Him. I hope you get a chance to enjoy this gift.

"There is a time for everything and a season for every activity under the heavens: a time to be born and a time to die, a time to plant and a time to uproot." **Ecclesiastes 3:1**

"Then the earth will yield its harvests, and God, our God, will richly bless us." **Psalm 67:6**

Wishing you a very joyful Lord's Day filled with blessings.

God's Plan

On this Lord's day, I find myself up in the early hours of the morning. There is something quite beautiful about the peaceful quietness I am surrounded with. It is a very special time to be in prayer and study scripture.

My mind has been on the "cross" this week, with Easter coming very soon. The sacrifice my Savior made on that cross at Calvary was the greatest gift ever given to me because, without it, I would be lost forever. He took all of my sin and shame upon Himself. He blessed me with the choice to repent and have my sins forgiven. My heart and soul burst with joy knowing I have that gift of Salvation. I pray that all of you choose to accept that gift and find that overwhelming joy.

"He himself bore our sins" in his body on the cross, so that we might die to sins and live for righteousness "by his wounds you have been healed." **1 Peter 2:24**

May you reflect on the cross at worship today.

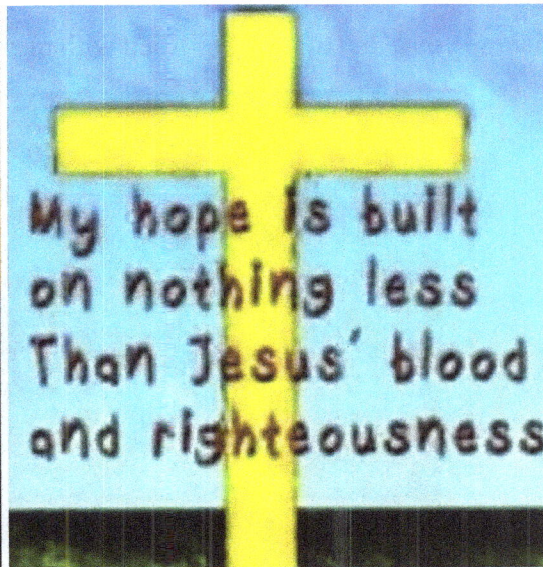

This was God's plan which he had made long ago; he knew all this would happen

Acts 2:23 (NCV)

My hope is built on nothing less Than Jesus' blood and righteousness

Roads Traveled

As I prepare for worship this morning, I am thinking about the many roads I have traveled in my 73 years. Some roads were rocky and difficult to travel. There have been roads that were all curves, roads that were dangerously steep and some that led to dead ends. These were roads with many potholes that were abound with all kinds of damage. These were roads I decided on my own to travel without asking God to lead my way.

I have learned that the best roads in life to travel are the ones that are guided by God's word. My prayer today is that the road we are on in life leads us to a time of worship on the Lord's Day.

"Then they said to him, 'please inquire of God to learn whether our journey is successful.' The priest answered them, "Go in peace. Your journey has the LORD's approval." **Judges 18:6-5**

"Ascribe to the LORD the glory due his name; worship the LORD in the splendor of his holiness." **Psalm 29:2**

Wishing you a day of worship filled with blessings.

Joy

As I prepare for worship on this Lord's Day, I feel joyous! It's always such a "JOY" to read scriptures pertaining to joy. Christian joy is a good feeling in the soul given to us by God. He lets us see the beauty of Christ in scripture and in the world. True joy is found deep within the heart and gives us a sense of gladness. Joy comes when we live in God's presence. Spiritual joy is a deep gladness that comes from knowing Jesus and having a relationship with God.

There aren't enough praises to be given to all the blessed Sunday school teachers who influenced my life and taught me joy. I give thanks to those who chose God's calling to teach the little ones.

"The precepts of the LORD are right, giving joy to the heart. The commands of the Lord are radiant, giving light to the eyes." **Psalm 19:8**

Wishing you a day of worship filled with joy deep in your heart.

Burdens

As I prepare for worship today, I am reminded that I sometimes carry a burden unnecessarily all by myself. God is glad to carry your burdens and give you daily strength.

At times, I can be slow at giving my burden to God. But, as soon as I put my trust in Him and give my burden to Him, it becomes lighter as He leads me.

There is also a burden of the spirit given by God, and such a burden is to have us intercede for other's burdens, and it is purposeful.

"Bear one another's burdens, and so fulfill the law of Christ." **Galatians 6:2**

"God is not unjust; he will not forget your work and the love you have shown him as you have helped his people and continue to help them." **Hebrews 6:10**

As you worship on this Lord's Day, I wish you a day of peace.

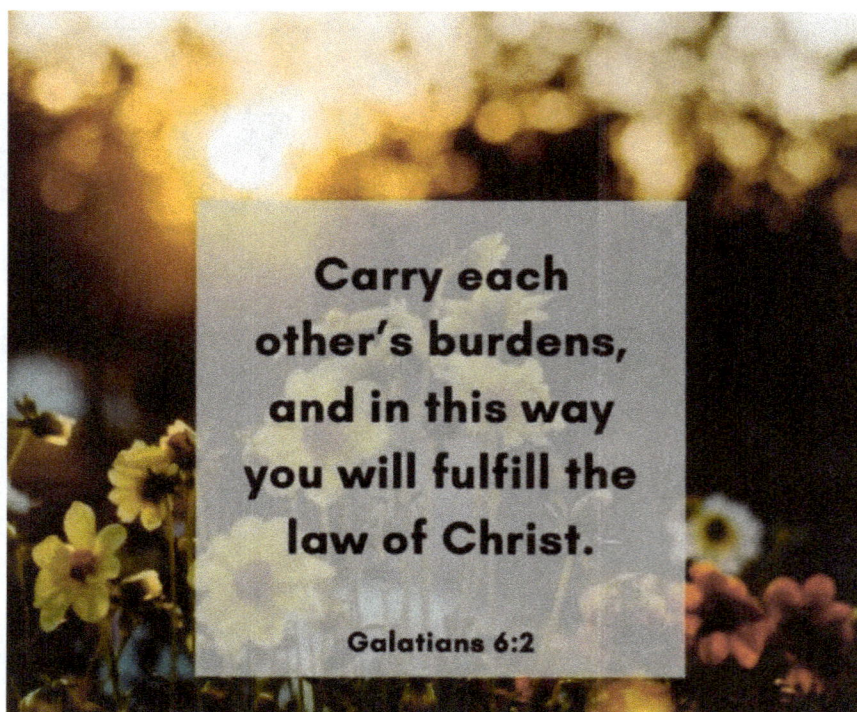

Carry each other's burdens, and in this way you will fulfill the law of Christ.

Galatians 6:2

Hymns

As I prepare for worship on this beautiful Lord's Day, I am sitting here listening to a CD of hymns, and they fill me with joy and precious memories. One hymn is "I Am Thine Own Way, Lord." It was the first hymn I played on the piano for church service, and I felt joy as my fingers touched those piano keys. I was self-taught to play, but I now know God taught me to play. Sacred music is the most precious of all music to me.

The hymns invite the Spirit of the Lord in me to create a feeling of reverence and provide a way for me to offer praises to the Lord. Some of the greatest sermons are preached by the singing of hymns.

"Let the word of Christ dwell in you richly; teach and admonish one another in all wisdom; and with gratitude in your hearts sing psalms, hymns and spiritual songs to God." **Colossians 3:16**

I wish each of you the joy of signing praises to the Lord as you worship today.

While I live will I praise the Lord I will sing praises unto my God while I have any being.

Psalm 146:2

This Little Light of Mine

On this day of worship, God is blessing us with a gloriously warm day, and I am grateful. Early this morning, in the peace and quiet of my alone time, I was reading the following Parable.

"...You are the Light of the world. A city set on a hill cannot be hidden. Nor do men light a lamp and put it under a bushel, but on a stand, and it gives light to all in the house. Let your light shine before men, that they may see your good works and give glory to your Father who is in heaven." **Matthew 5:14-16**

After reading this, I remembered that, as a child, we would sing a song in Sunday School that would bring me so much joy... *"This Little Light of Mine."*

It is not that we ought to be the light. It's that we are the light. We are meant to shine by doing good works that glorify God. It is the nature of light to dispel the darkness. Whether you are timid or outgoing, you are called to be the light to the people around you.

I hope you let your light shine as you worship today.

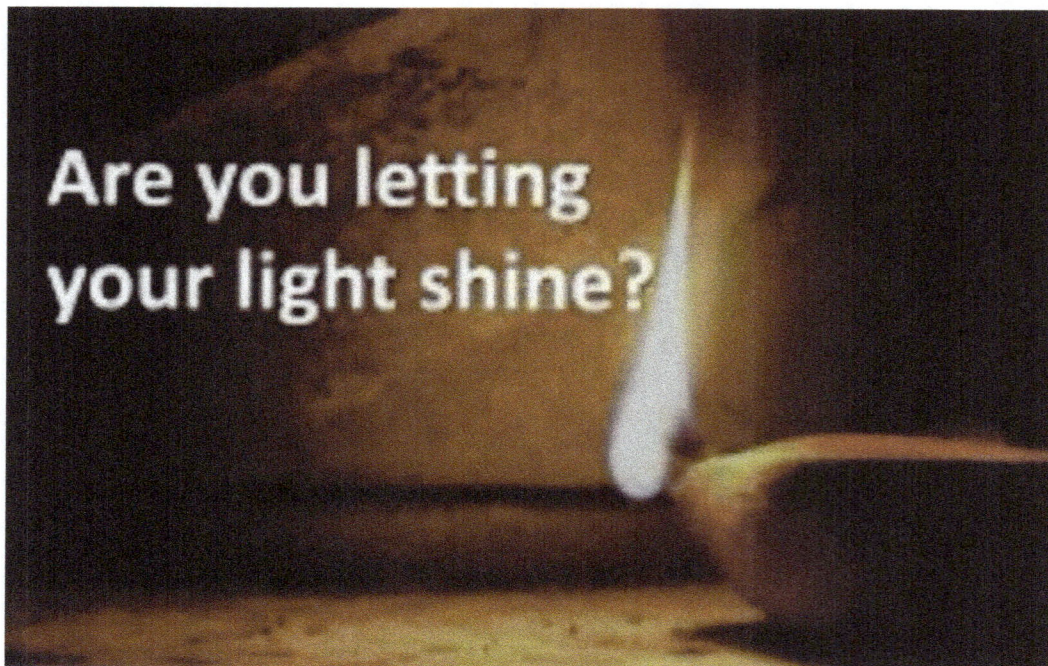

It is Well with My Soul

I have been granted another Lord's Day, and I am grateful. Life is sweet and good, but it can also be very hard at times. God did not promise a stress-free life, but He promised that He would be with us every step of the way.

> *"Beloved, I pray that all may go well with you and that you may be in good health, just as it is well with your soul."*
> **3 John 2**

> *"When the cares of my heart are many, your consolations cheer my soul."* **Psalm 93:19**

The soul is the essence of who we are, and it includes our mind, our will, emotions, desires and passions. It's the connection between our material body and our spiritual self. Is it well with your soul?

Wishing you a day filled with blessings and a life that is well with your soul.

Tithing

Thank you, Lord, for another Sabbath to worship. I am thinking about how much God has given me and how much I have given back to Him. Christians still believe that everything they have comes from God, so it's only natural that they "tithe" a portion of their earnings in thanksgiving to the God they serve. The 10% tithe is only the beginning of what generosity could look like for the Church.

The verse about tithing one-tenth of your income is found in,

"A tithe of everything from the land, whether grain from the soil or fruit from the trees, belongs to the Lord; it is holy to the Lord." **Leviticus 27:30**

"Each of you should give what you have decided in your heart to give, not reluctantly or under compulsion, for God loves a cheerful giver. And God is able to bless you abundantly, so that in all things at all times, having all that you need, so that in all things at all times, having all that you need, you will abound in every good work." *2* **Corinthians 9:7-8**

Wishing you a day of worship with a generous heart.

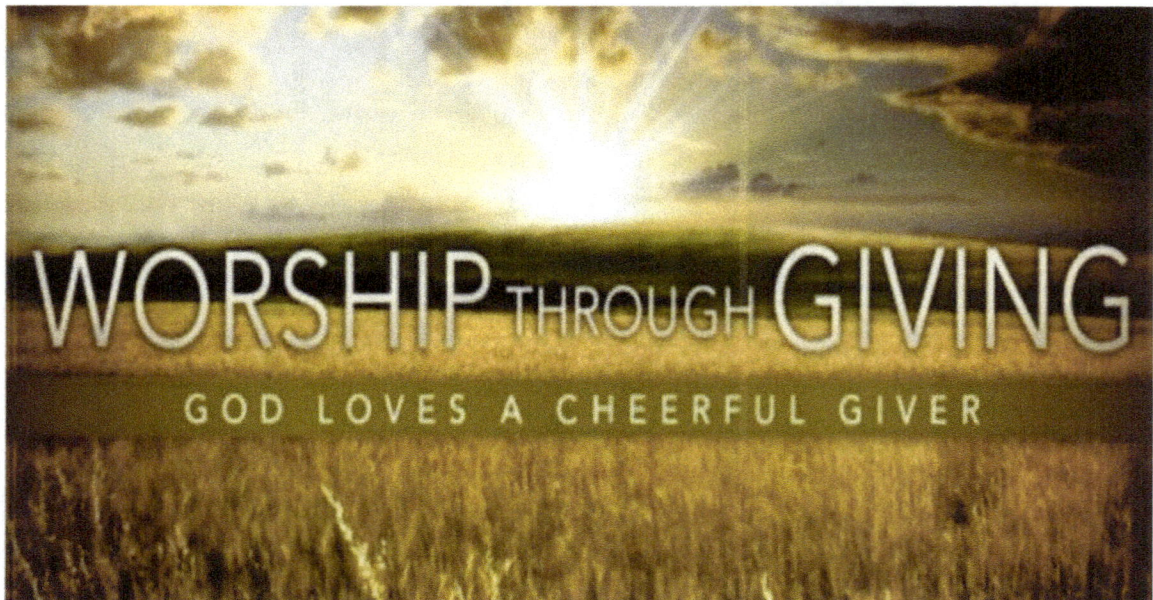

WORSHIP THROUGH GIVING

GOD LOVES A CHEERFUL GIVER

Sunday School

I am so grateful to be able to worship on another Lord's Day. I am enjoying memories of Sunday School when I was a child. I was blessed to have Christian parents who also taught children's Sunday School. That is where I first learned many of the stories of the Bible. I was given knowledge of the Bible, kindness, love and Christian fellowship with other children. I remember the children's worship songs, and I still sing them occasionally. As an adult, I was blessed to teach in children's Sunday School, and I believe that as a teacher, you hold one of the most important ministries in church. It is a stepping stone to Salvation for many children.

Those who teach children's Sunday School have a very important responsibility. Some children come in with all the answers, from teachings at home, and to others, the teacher is the first godly face they have seen. When you teach Sunday School, you have the chance to influence their entire life for the sake of the Gospel.

"And all thy children shall be taught of the Lord, and great shall be the peace of thy children." **Isaiah 54:13**

"Train up a child in the way he should go: and when he is old, he will not depart from it." **Proverbs 22:6**

Let us keep lifting up our Sunday School in our prayers. Wherever you worship today, I wish you joy and blessings.

Thankful

As I prepare for worship this morning, I am thinking about thankfulness and gratefulness. There's a beautiful cycle in giving God thanks. I have learned that the more I thank Him, the more I see Him working in me and around me. Gratitude helps me sense God's presence, His personal care and His perfect timing.

Gratitude isn't just the feeling I get after something good happens to me. It's a way of thinking that has taken the practice to make it part of my everyday behavior. It's often easy to forget many of the little things I have to be grateful for in my life, but it's important not to take anything for granted.

"Rejoice always, pray continually, give thanks in all circumstances; for this is God's will for you in Christ Jesus." In this verse, Paul encourages us to be thankful in all situations, even when they are difficult. **1 Thessalonians 5:18**

I wish each of you a day of worship filled with gratitude and thankfulness.

Thank You God for everything in my life. The good & bad. Some were Blessings & some were Lessons! ☺

Too Busy

As I prepared for worship this morning, I was reminiscing about a time when my kids were small and Sunday mornings were a complete rush to get everyone ready for church and how easy it would have been to just sleep in. But then I would think of the price that was paid for the blessing of going freely to worship at my choice of church. The feeling of walking into the Lord's House with my family was always so rewarding.

Most of the time, we find ourselves rushing around, trying to do the things that need to be done and missing out on the many blessings Jesus has for us. When we allow ourselves to get too busy, we don't take time to slow down and remember the relationship we have with God. God wants us to spend time each day to renew our relationship with Him. I hope I am never too busy to spend time worshipping our Lord.

> *"But an hour is coming, and now is, when the true worshippers shall worship the Father in spirit and truth; for such people the Father seeks to be His worshippers..."*
> **John 4:23**

Hoping you make time to worship today and that your day is filled with blessings.

The gospel is too important, eternity is too long and life is too short for us to be too busy.

Peace

As I prepare for worship this morning, my mind is and has been focused on the wars and the troubles around the world as well as in our own country. It seems that there are protests, war and persecution all over the world and even in our own Country.

To have peace in my own heart, I know I need to humble myself in prayer, turn to God, open His word and trust what He says. I know I need to adjust my heart to His truth, not allowing the world's appearance to steer me. I know I need to lean not on my own understanding or self-doubting but on God's specific words and promises to me in the Bible.

"My times are in your hand; Deliver me from the hand of my enemies and from those who persecute me." **Psalm 31:15**

Please be in prayer with me for those so desperately trying to escape war and persecution. Wishing everyone a day of praise and worship that brings peace to your heart.

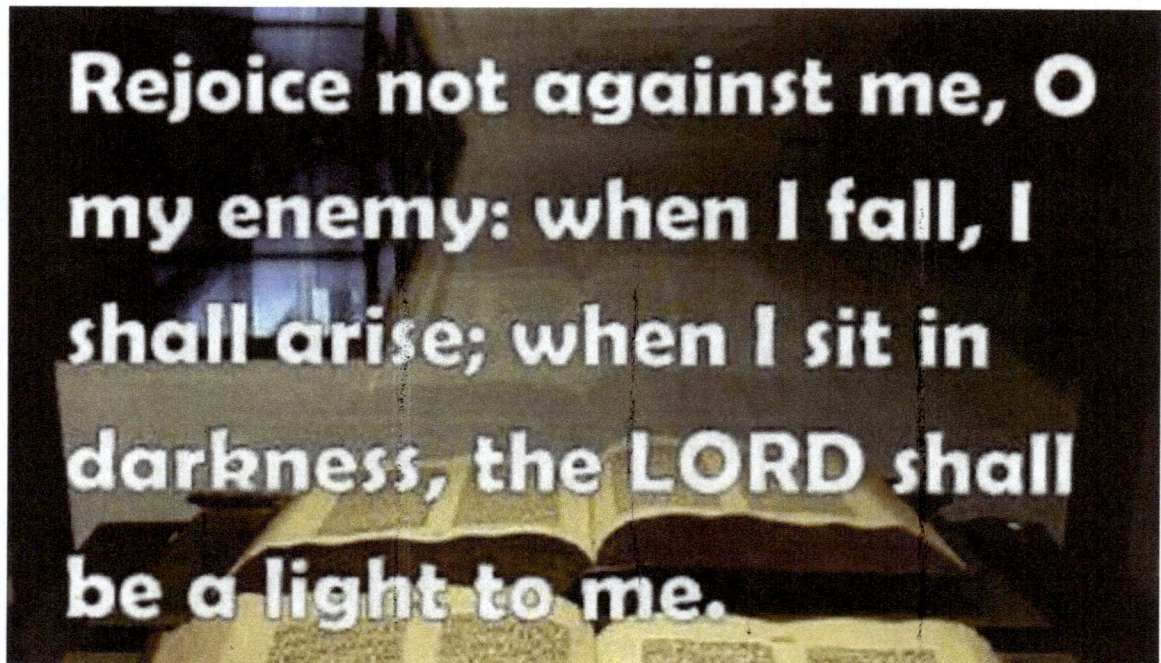

Rejoice not against me, O my enemy: when I fall, I shall arise; when I sit in darkness, the LORD shall be a light to me.

My Bucket is Full

As I prepare for worship this morning, I am reminded of an email from a friend about a bucket list and all that I wanted to fill out. The list of unfulfilled wishes was quite long. I gave it a lot of thought because my bucket was already full and overflowing with blessings.

I have seen hard times, lean times, illness and grief, just like each of you. But my bucket is already filled with gratitude and thankfulness because God has always carried me through those times. My bucket is mostly filled with good gifts from God that far outweigh the bad. I have learned to be content and happy with what God has provided for me. I know whatever my future holds, God will continue to fill my bucket with His love and plans for me.

"Not that I speak in need, for I have learned, whatever state I am in, to be content."
Philippians 4:11

Wishing you a day of worship filled with thankfulness, contentment and blessings.

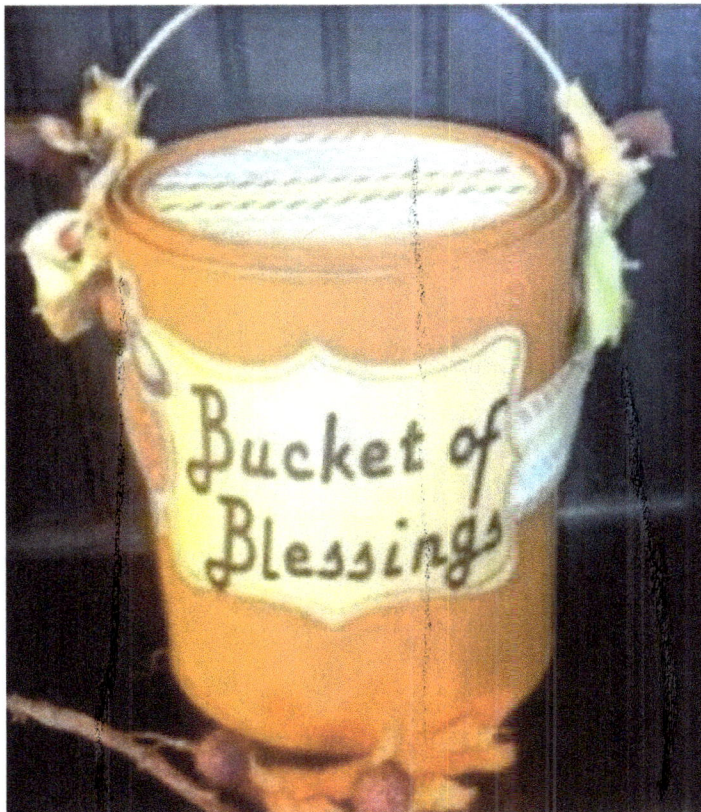

Conquer Evil

As I prepare for worship today, like most of us, I grow tired of seeing tragic events, and they weigh heavy on my heart. As Christians, we must stop standing idly by while satan is building his army all around us. We have allowed worldly lifestyles to replace Godly lifestyles.

So many homes are broken. So many people with no morals. Many children are not receiving any spiritual training. We have to stand up against evil and those who seek to destroy everything that is good and from God. We need to let our prayers and lifestyles serve as testimonies to those who are lost and seeking peace in their lives.

"Do not be overcome with evil, but overcome evil with good." **Romans 12:21**

"Therefore, take up the whole armor of God, that you will be able to withstand in the evil day, and having done all, to stand firm." **Ephesians 6:13**

My prayer today is that I can rebuke the things Satan has made acceptable in today's world and stand firm for God in all things.

Wishing you a day of worship that brings you peace and is filled with blessings.

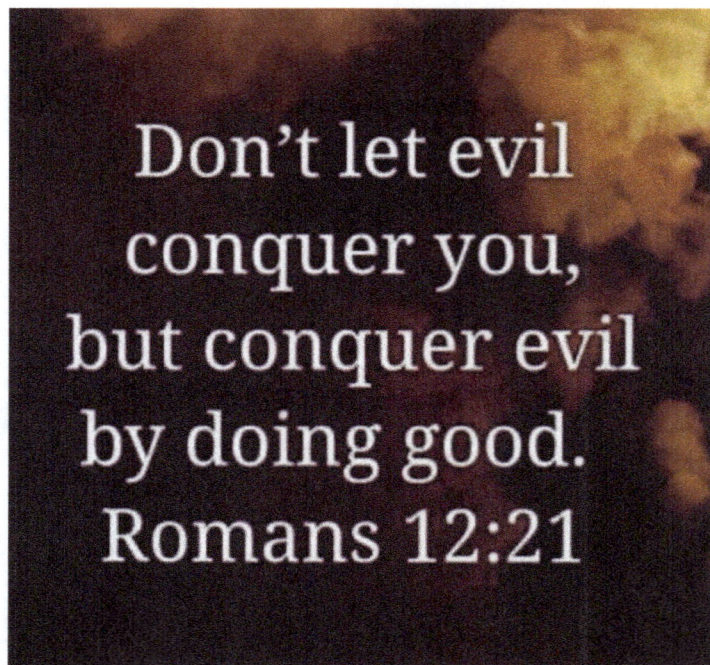

Don't let evil conquer you, but conquer evil by doing good. Romans 12:21

Canvas of Life

God has granted me yet another Lord's Day to worship Him, and I am grateful. This week, my husband gave me a gift—a new painting easel that he lovingly assembled.

It is beautifully made of dark furniture quality wood. It can be adjusted to any size I desire and even has two drawers to hold my supplies.

As I admired it early this morning, these thoughts came to mind. I began to compare the easel, which is the foundation upon holding my blank canvas for me to paint what I desire. As I looked at it, I thought this easel was like my life. Built from God's word, I have been given a strong foundation. On that foundation, God has given me free will to choose what I place on the canvas of life. It is up to me to fill my life with colors that are pleasing to God.

"For no one can lay a foundation other than that which is laid, which is Jesus Christ."
1 Corinthians 3:11

Wishing you a joyful day of worship and a day filled with blessings.

Old Country Church

I am blessed to see another Lord's Day, and I am grateful. I saw a photo of a very old church, and it made me think of how people traveled there for Sunday worship service. Maybe they came by horse and buggy or walked some distance. I wondered about the difficulties they faced just to get to that church to worship. I thought of all the souls that found salvation in that old church, the weddings, the baptisms and the funerals. I have read that it was customary to gather for a meal and fellowship after the service. I wondered why that church died. Did they build a new one, did the people move away, or did they get too busy to go to church like many people today?

Just think how easy it is for us to jump in our car and get to a church close by. If it is hot, we enjoy air-conditioned auditoriums, and when it is cold, we enjoy heaters in our churches. And yet today, sadly, some find it too much trouble to attend church. I hope I never find myself too busy or too lazy to worship on the Lord's Day.

"God is spirit, and those who worship him must worship in spirit and truth." **John 4:24**

Wishing you a day of worship filled with fellowship and blessings

Hope

As I was preparing for worship on this Lord's Day, I looked out the window and saw the hope of Spring. Wild green onions are poking out of the brown grass, and the crocus is in bloom. The sun is shining, and the birds are singing. There are small buds on the trees that will soon bring glorious colors of green. God's beauty in nature brings forth hope.

Hope is found in the promises God has given us. We can find so much hope in Scripture through the gift of eternal life made possible through His son, Jesus Christ. No matter what trials, temptations or pain we may suffer, we can always hold onto the hope God extends to us.

"May the God of hope fill you with all joy and peace as you trust in him, so that you may overflow with hope by the power of the Holy Spirit." **Romans 15:13**

Wishing you a very blessed day as you worship our God of Hope today.

Always put your hope in GOD

Growing Old

I am grateful that God has granted me another Lord's Day to worship and praise him. I am closing in on 74 years of age, and I hope God has many more years here in his plan for me. There is so much I still want to do and see. I would love to see a great-grandchild. I would love to share Jesus with more people. I have loved ones whom I want to see receiving salvation. I have life experiences I want to share. Over the years, God has taught me many valuable lessons that I still have to share.

Until God calls me home, I hope to live my life according to this Scripture...

"But none of these things move me, neither count I my life dear unto myself, so that I might finish my course with joy, and the ministry, which I have received of the Lord Jesus, to testify the gospel of the grace of God." **Acts 20:24**

I wish you a day of meaningful worship and a day filled with God's blessings.

> *My only aim is to finish the* **race** *and complete the* **task** *the* **Lord Jesus** *has given me—*
>
> *The task of testifying to the good news of* **God's Grace.**

Knowing God

As I prepare for worship this morning, I am thinking about someone who is really a good person, who is kind, does good works, and who is generous. But, this person claims to be an Agnostic. An agnostic believes it is impossible to know if God exists. I believe we need to be in prayer for those who claim they are Agnostic; they either believe or not. There is no sitting on the fence about this. There is a great difference between knowing about God and truly knowing— you have a relationship with God and that you know you are a Child of God.

"For it is believing in your heart that you are made right with God, and it is by openly declaring your faith that you are saved." **Romans 10:10**

My prayer is that I never miss the opportunity to be a witness for my Savior and that I never am the cause for someone to turn away from God.

Wishing you a day of worship that is pleasing to our Lord and brings joy to your heart.

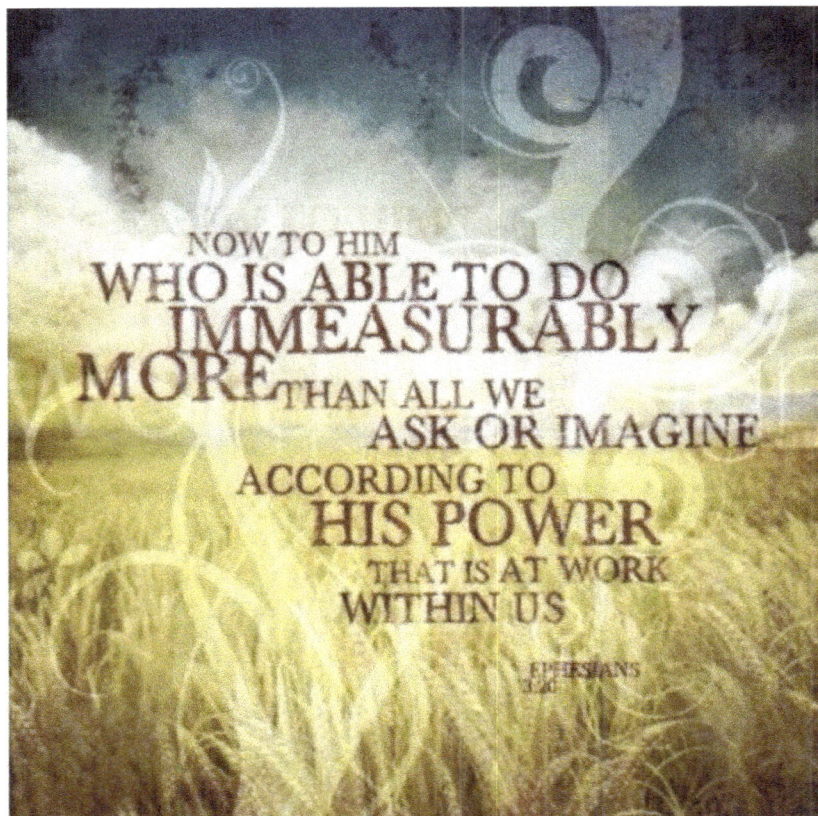

NOW TO HIM WHO IS ABLE TO DO IMMEASURABLY MORE THAN ALL WE ASK OR IMAGINE ACCORDING TO HIS POWER THAT IS AT WORK WITHIN US

EPHESIANS

In the Garden

I am grateful that I have been granted another Lord's day. As usual, I peeked out outside to see if everything was as it should be. What I found this morning was the beauty God created from the lush green grass and trees. My lilies are just about to bloom, and they are surrounded by small pink flowers. Who else? Only God created something so beautiful as flowers. The sun is shining, the birds are singing, and the cicadas are blasting their song. I began humming one of my favorites..."*Come to The Garden Alone.*" I hope you are familiar with this hymn.

One day in March 1912, C. Austin Miles, who composed this hymn, picked up his Bible. It had fallen open to John, chapter 20. He found in that chapter the story of Mary's coming to the garden to visit the tomb of Jesus. As she looked into the tomb, her heart sank because he wasn't there. This inspired composer Miles to write this beloved hymn.

"Flowers appear on the earth; the season of singing has come; the cooing of doves are heard in our land."
Solomon 2:12

I hope we all find time to spend alone with God in the beauty of what He has created. I wish you joy as you worship and praise God today and that your day is filled with blessings.

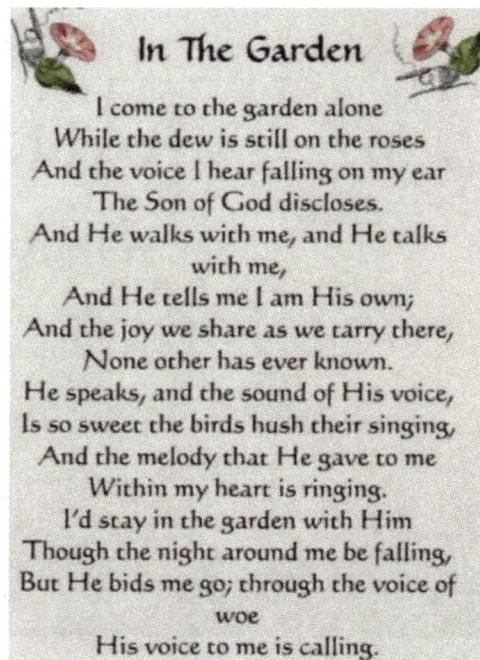

In The Garden

I come to the garden alone
While the dew is still on the roses
And the voice I hear falling on my ear
The Son of God discloses.
And He walks with me, and He talks with me,
And He tells me I am His own;
And the joy we share as we tarry there,
None other has ever known.
He speaks, and the sound of His voice,
Is so sweet the birds hush their singing,
And the melody that He gave to me
Within my heart is ringing.
I'd stay in the garden with Him
Though the night around me be falling,
But He bids me go; through the voice of woe
His voice to me is calling.

Count Your Blessings

As I am preparing for worship this morning, I have been thinking about times that I find myself drifting towards the comparative structure of material things, allowing social media feeds and nightly news to determine how satisfied I am with the status quo of my life. These are times when I find that counting my blessings turns my thoughts quickly around. Counting our blessings takes our focus off of what we do not have and puts it on God, who makes all things possible.

Counting our blessings makes us happy for the good things we have. Counting our blessings strengthens our journey. Thank you, Lord, for blessing me much more than I deserve. I love the hymn *"Count Your Blessings, name them one by one, And it will surprise you what the Lord hath done."*

"Shout for joy to God, all the Earth! Sing the glory of his name; make his praise glorious. Say to God, "How awesome are your deeds." **Psalm 66**

"Bless the Lord, O my soul and forget not all his benefits." **Psalms 103:2**

Wishing you a day filled with blessings and a heart filled with praise and thankfulness.

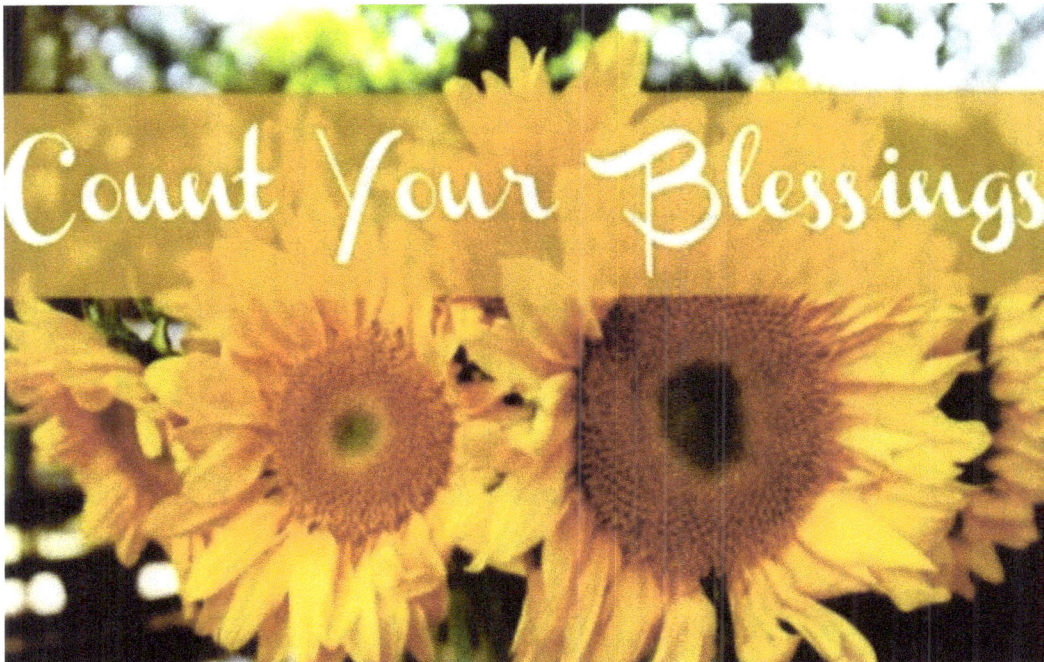

Lies

As I prepare for worship this morning, I feel ashamed of a lie I told. I told myself it was just a little old white lie, but I know better because God hates lies. I have asked for forgiveness, but I wonder how many times in my life I have told little white lies. Well, I am calling them little white lies, but there is no such thing because, in God's eyes, a lie is a lie. In today's world, it has become of the utmost importance to know a lie when you hear it, to know right from wrong and to know good from evil.

That being said, it's not always easy to arm yourself with the Word of God! You know how it is... life gets busy, the devil is nipping at your heels, and it seems like worldly influences crowd out your best intentions.

"Lying lips are an abomination to the Lord, but those that deal truly are His delight." **Proverbs 12:22**

"Therefore, put on every piece of God's armor so you will be able to resist the enemy in the time of evil. Then, after the battle, you will still be standing firm." **Ephesians 6:13**

Wishing you a day of worship filled with blessings.

A LIE DOESN'T BECOME TRUTH, WRONG DOESN'T BECOME RIGHT, AND EVIL DOESN'T BECOME GOOD, JUST BECAUSE IT'S ACCEPTED BY A MAJORITY.

God Sees All Time

As I am preparing for worship on this Lord's Day, it seems like time is passing me by at warp speed. Lately, I have been thinking a lot about how I wish I could relive some days of my past. Just like everyone, I have some regrets and wish I could have some do-overs. Maybe this is how people feel when they are in the winter season of their life. I am learning that there is still much to do in God's plan for me. Aging in the Bible is said to be a sign of experience. I take great comfort in knowing that God promises His continued love and concern for me.

God sees all of time from the beginning to the end, and He tells us the same thing He told Israel back then. God sees all time.

"Forget the former things; do not dwell on the past. See, I am doing a new thing."
Isaiah 43:18

"I will be your God throughout your lifetime—until your hair is white with age. I made you, and I will take care of you. I will carry you along and save you. **Isaiah 46:4**

Wishing you a day of worship that fills your heart with joy and blessings.

Praying for Others

As I prepare for worship this morning, I am thinking about how long my prayer list for others has been lately. When we say we will pray for someone and we just let the phrase fall out of our mouth and not follow through, it is the same as saying good luck to them, and our words are empty and meaningless. The word "praying" by itself has no power. It is only when a follower of Jesus goes to Him in prayer on someone's behalf that things begin to move.

Many times in life, people have prayed for you without your knowledge; possibly, those prayers have saved you many times. Always pray for others who can't pray for themselves because others prayed for you when you couldn't. Praying for others is an unselfish expression of love.

> *"For this reason, since we heard about you, we have not stopped praying for you. We continually ask God to fill you with the knowledge of his will through all the wisdom and understanding that the Spirit gives."* **Colossians 1:9**

> *"Carry each other's burdens, and in this way, you will fulfill the law of Christ."* **Galatians 6:2**

Wishing you a day of worship filled with joy and blessings.

Free to Worship

As I prepare for worship this morning, I do so with a grateful heart because I am free to praise God where and when I want to every day. I am free to carry a Bible, wear a cross, and pray anywhere at any time. In a startling number of countries, the freedom to worship Jesus, gather in churches and peacefully practice one's faith is under assault.

Sadly, the turmoil in our Country today threatens our future to worship freely. As Christians, we must never take this freedom to worship God for granted. I pray that we each take time to worship today and teach our children what a privilege and gift it is to do so.

"Give unto the LORD the glory due unto his name; worship the LORD in the beauty of holiness." **Psalms 29:2**

Wishing everyone a day of worship filled with many blessings.

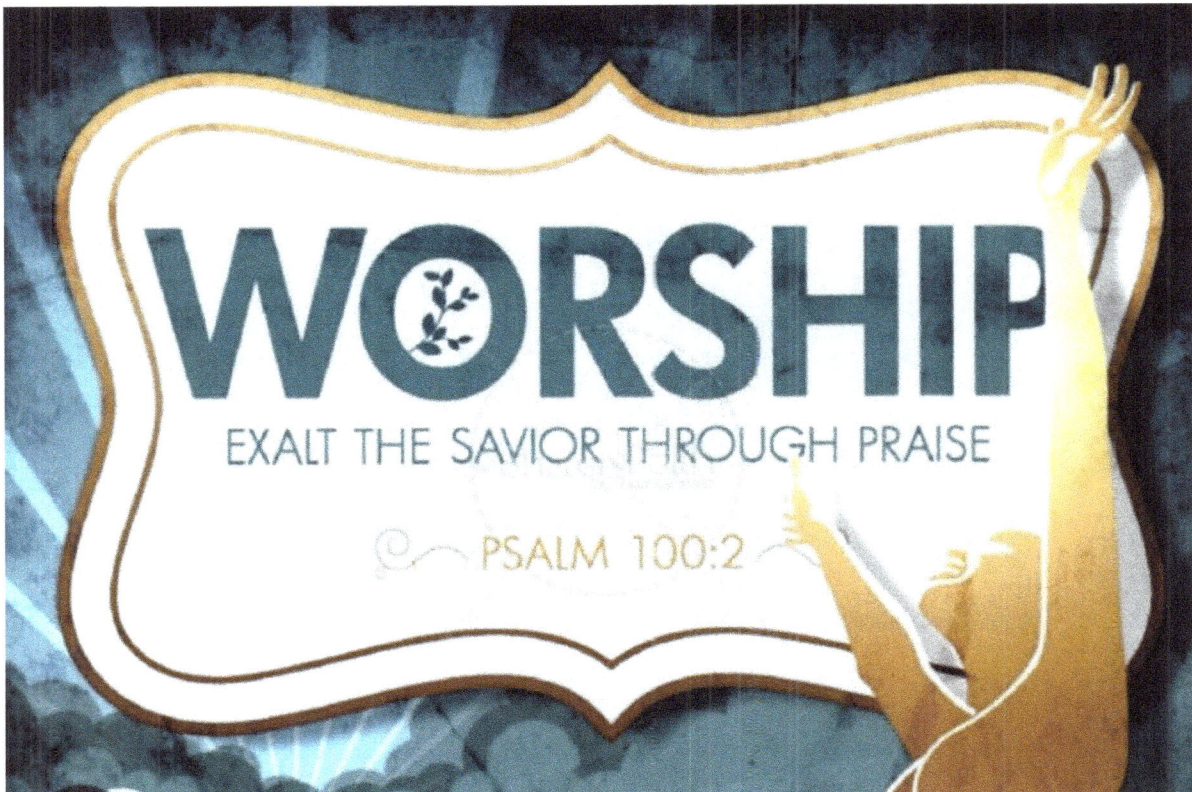

Time is Fleeting

As I prepare for worship today, I am thinking about the world around us. So many people are so wrapped up in themselves, politics and their own pleasure that they don't have time for God.

> ""*This also, that in the last days, perilous times shall come. For men shall be lovers of their own selves, covetous, boasters, proud, blasphemers, disobedient to parents, unthankful, unholy, traitors, heady, high, indeed, lovers of pleasures more than lovers of God; having a form of godliness, but denying the power thereof: from such turn away.*" **2 Timothy 3:1-5**

Are we not seeing these traits in mankind today? So because of these traits, man has turned his back on God. We must do, with urgency, everything we can to bring Jesus to everyone we can. Time is fleeting.

Please pray that we may not miss any opportunity to share Jesus and the Gospel.

May you have a day of worship filled with praise and joy.

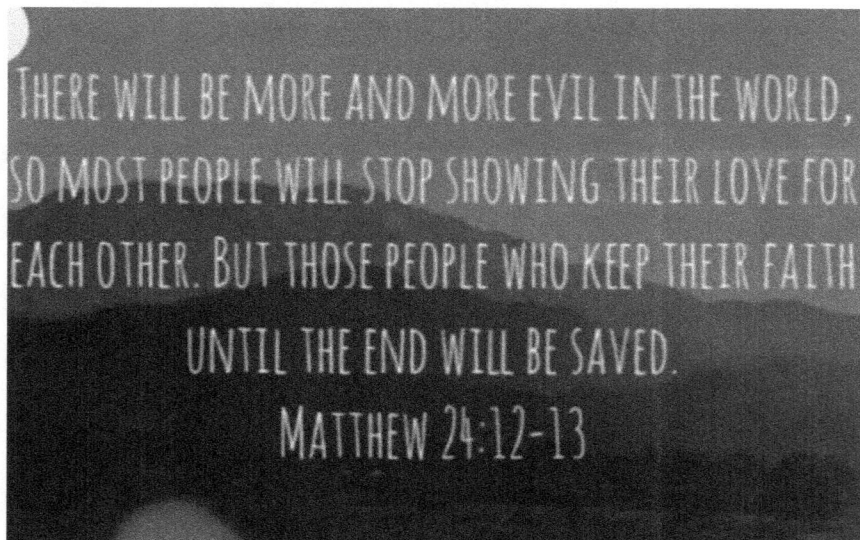

THERE WILL BE MORE AND MORE EVIL IN THE WORLD, SO MOST PEOPLE WILL STOP SHOWING THEIR LOVE FOR EACH OTHER. BUT THOSE PEOPLE WHO KEEP THEIR FAITH UNTIL THE END WILL BE SAVED. MATTHEW 24:12-13

Speaking with Kindness

God has granted me another Lord's Day to worship. I learned a new word, and it is POLYGLOTS, which means speaking in many languages. I am not a Polyglot. I only speak English and a tad bit of Spanish. But this word, polyglots, made me think of one language which everyone all over the world can speak, and that is kindness. As Christians, our kindness reflects the heart of God. Kindness is the will to do good, just as Jesus shows kindness for us.

For the perfect example of kindness, we need to look no farther than Jesus. Kindness is selfless, compassionate and merciful. Kindness is the fruit of the Spirit, along with love, joy and peace.

"Whoever is kind to the poor lends to the Lord, and he will repay them for what they have done."
Proverbs 19:17

On this day of worship, may we all show kindness as our Lord has shown to us.

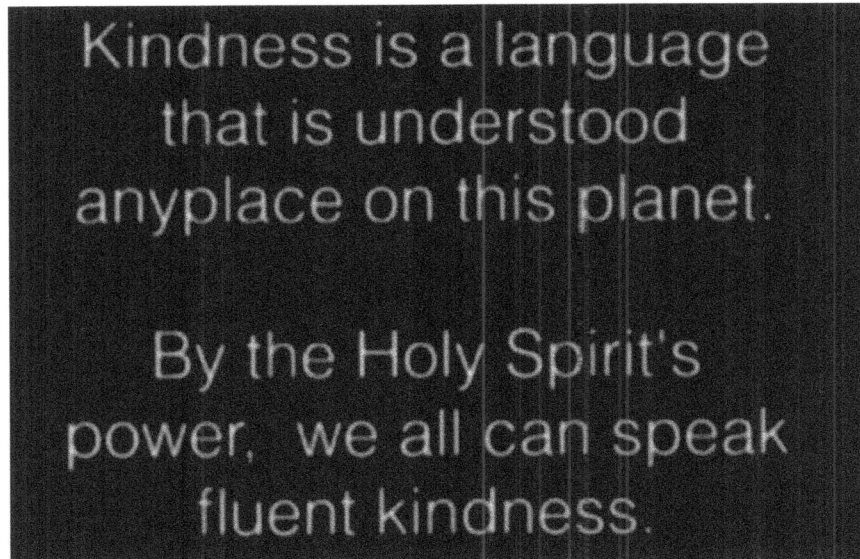

Kindness is a language
that is understood
anyplace on this planet.

By the Holy Spirit's
power, we all can speak
fluent kindness.

Blessed Assurance

As I prepare for worship on this Lord's Day, I am thinking about my parents, whom God has called home to Heaven. I know they are rejoicing there because I have been given a blessed assurance. To have blessed assurance means to be certain, confident and free from doubt. Blessed assurance is a holy and sacred confidence. It is an unshakeable certainty of the truth that Jesus is mine, and I am His. I know that He is my Savior and Lord forever.

I know these five assurances from God: Assurance of salvation, assurance of answered prayer, assurance of victory over death, assurance of forgiveness and assurance of guidance. There is a beautiful hymn, *"Blessed Assurance,"* and I hope you are familiar with it.

"Let us draw near to God with a sincere heart and with the full assurance that faith brings."
Hebrews 10:22

Wishing you a wonderful day of worship, and hope your heart is filled with blessed assurance.

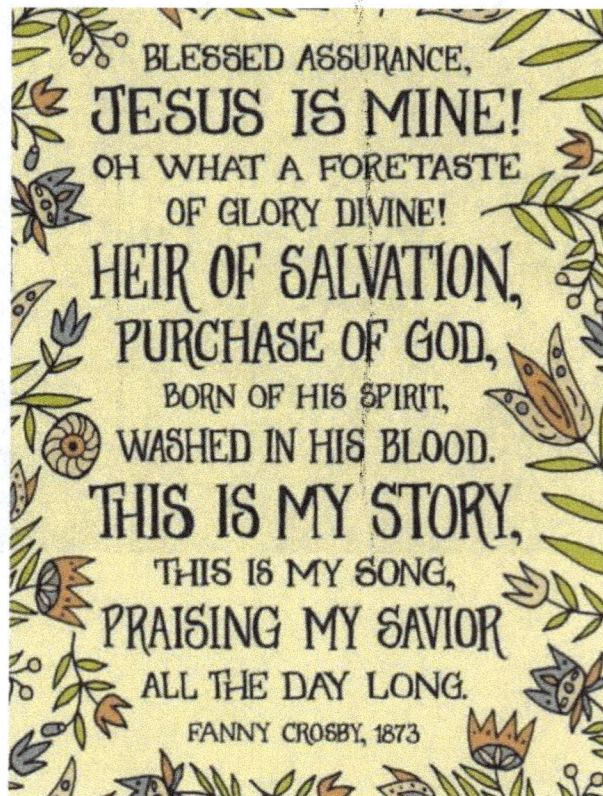

BLESSED ASSURANCE, JESUS IS MINE! OH WHAT A FORETASTE OF GLORY DIVINE! HEIR OF SALVATION, PURCHASE OF GOD, BORN OF HIS SPIRIT, WASHED IN HIS BLOOD. THIS IS MY STORY, THIS IS MY SONG, PRAISING MY SAVIOR ALL THE DAY LONG. FANNY CROSBY, 1873

Amazing Grace

My first thought as I prepare for worship is grace. God has shown me Grace all the days of my life. Grace means to get something you do not deserve, and I am thankful for God's grace, for He has given it to me when I did not deserve it; he gave it more times than I could count.

Saving grace is the grace God gives to sinners to influence their hearts and turn them to Jesus. God shows us many kinds of grace, such as saving grace, sanctifying grace, sharing grace, and serving grace.

I am reminded of this scripture...

"But to each one of us, grace has been given as Christ apportioned it." **Ephesians 4:7**

Grace is God's gift to us of forgiveness, acceptance, and love. It is Grace that draws us to him. There is no way we can earn grace. God's gift of grace to us is just that, a gift.

There is a hymn I am sure you are all familiar with, *"Amazing Grace."*

As you worship today, remember God's amazing Grace and a day filled with blessings.

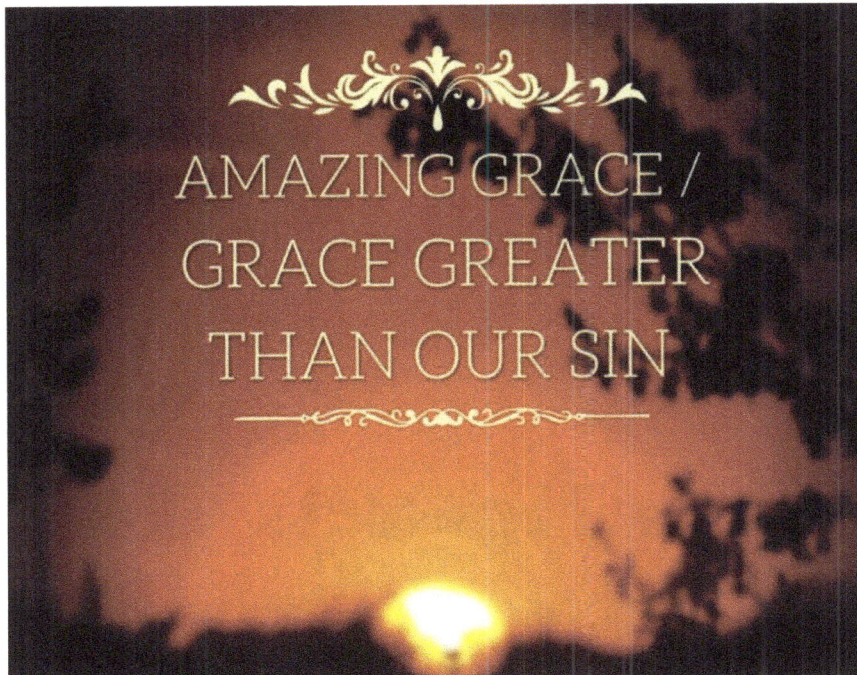

AMAZING GRACE /
GRACE GREATER
THAN OUR SIN

Mercy

It is time for worship today, and I am thankful that God has granted me this day. Mercy is on my mind this morning. God's mercy is shown by sending Jesus Christ to give his life on the cross for our sins. His mercy is the act of compassion, kindness, and forgiveness, especially to those who have sinned. Jesus showed mercy by healing, comforting, and caring for those in need. As in the parable, when we are truly repentant, God shows us mercy and welcomes us with open arms. Mercy is an extension of God's love, and it is a way for him to draw us closer to him and invite us to a closer relationship with him.

We need to thank God every day in our prayers, for which he showed mercy to us. I do not deserve mercy, and yet God grants me mercy every day of my life. God has the power to punish me, but he chooses to show me his gift of mercy.

"The steadfast love of the Lord never ceases: his mercies never come to an end; they are new every morning; great is your faithfulness." **Lamentations 3:22-23**

"For judgement is without mercy to one who has shown no mercy. Mercy triumphs over judgement." **James 3:13**

As you worship today, I wish you a day of praise filled with blessings.

"Its a good thing God's Mercy is new every morning, because I have used up all of Yesterday's supply!"

Reading God's Word

As I prepare for worship, I am reading from my CSB Bible In A Year. I like this Bible for daily devotion and time with God. It is good for studying the Bible. Each day has passages from the Old Testament, Palms, Proverbs and the New Testament. It also has a commentary and a prayer for each day. Although the King James Version is beautiful, sometimes it is hard to understand. There is a NIV Bible that is written in today's language and may be easier to understand at times. I would suggest that someone who is new to God's word to start with the New Testament—four Gospels.

The importance of reading and studying the Bible is that we learn who God is, and it contains His message about all the things that give our life meaning. Reading the Bible helps us to grow closer to God. There is no denying that being a better Christian starts with reading the Word of God every day. It is good to pray and ask God for help in understanding it and how to apply it to our lives.

"Until I come, devote yourself to public reading of the Scripture, to preaching and teaching." **1 Timothy 4:13**

As you worship today, I wish you joy and blessings in God's word.

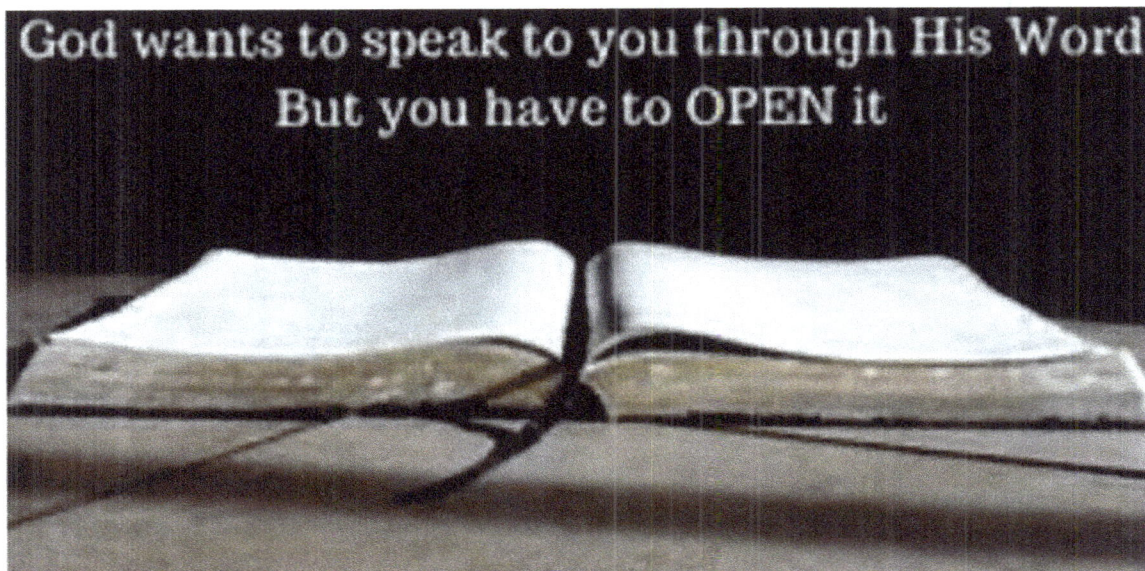

God wants to speak to you through His Word
But you have to OPEN it

Forgiveness

As I am preparing for worship today, I am watching raindrops sliding down my window. They remind me of the tears I have shed when someone has hurt me.

I have to admit my first thought has not been forgiveness. I have found out that holding onto a grudge only hurts me. There have been times in my life I have asked God to unburden me of that hurt and find forgiveness. Each time, He answered my prayer, changed my heart so I could give forgiveness, and lifted the hurt and the burden. When I grasp how little I deserve God's forgiveness, then I become more willing to forgive others. Unforgiveness is a poison to our soul.

"Do not judge, and you will not be judged. Do not condemn, and you will not be condemned. Forgive, and you will be forgiven." **Luke 6:37**

I am forever grateful for God's forgiveness. According to the Bible, God's forgiveness is limitless and available to anyone who asks for it, so there should be no limit to our forgiveness of others.

"Jesus said, 'I do not say to you, up to seven 1imes, but up to seventy times seven.'" **Matthew 18:22**

God has granted me another glorious Lord's Day to worship Him and I am grateful. Wishing you a day of worship filled with blessings.

Bear with each other and forgive one another if any of you has a grievance against someone. Forgive as the Lord forgave you.

Colossians 3:13 NIV

Testimonies

Praise God, he has granted me another day to worship, and I am grateful. I am thinking about what giving our testimonies means. Our testimonies are about who we are and what we did, and more about who Jesus is and what he has done for us. I was saved when I was 11, and I used to think my testimony, being saved as a child, was somehow worthless. It was not stirring like those who came to know Jesus through some tragedy or addiction. I wondered if my simple story of coming to salvation as a child mattered. Would I ever be able to affect anyone with my faith since my testimony was so unextraordinary? Since then, I have learned that no testimony is ever pathetic or worthless.

Our testimonies are less about who we were and what we did and more about who Christ is and what He has done for us. I can be a light for Jesus, no matter that I feel that my testimony is insignificant to other Christian testimonies. God has given each of us a story that He can work through every day.

"Let your light shine before others, so that they may see your good works and give glory to your Father who is in Heaven." **Matthew 6:16**

May you worship today with joy and love in your heart.

Seek out opportunities to share your testimony

Worry

As I prepare for worship today, my mind is worrying. Worry is something I have struggled with. I have learned much about worrying and anxiety from the Bible. God puts a lot about this in the Bible. The Bible provides encouragement as well as practical examples of how to work on this with God's help.

"Do not be anxious about anything, but in every situation, by prayer and petition, with thanksgiving, present your requests to God. And the peace of God, which transcends all understanding, will guard your hearts and your minds in Christ Jesus." **Philippians 4:6-7**

"Therefore, do not be anxious about tomorrow, for tomorrow will be anxious for itself. Sufficient for the day is its own trouble." **Matthew 26:34**

Instead of worrying, praying and having a sense of God's wholeness, everything coming together for good will come and settle you down. There are times when I spend a great deal of time in prayer about something worrisome, but God always gives me relief and comfort.

Wishing you a day of worship filled with joy and a day filled with blessings.

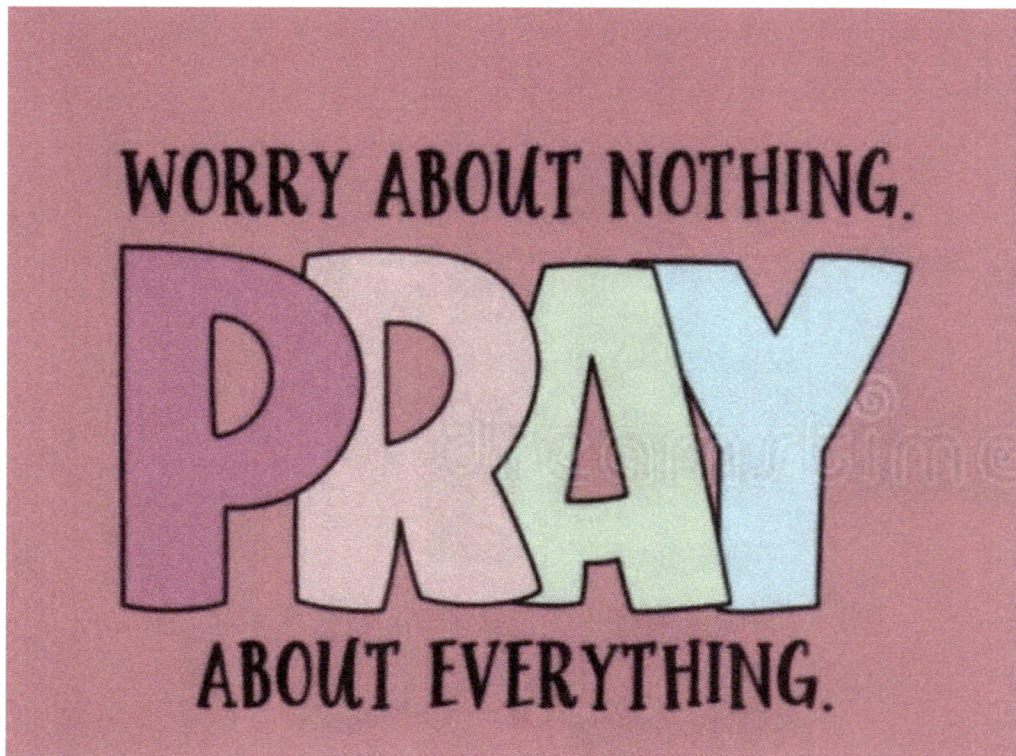

WORRY ABOUT NOTHING. PRAY ABOUT EVERYTHING.

Encouragement

God has granted me another day to worship, and I am grateful. Encouragement is an important part of the Christian life; many times in the New Testament, Christians are told to encourage one another. The Bible names encouragement as a spiritual gift, and I believe that, as Christians, we all have been given this gift. Although it is easy to use, it has also become somewhat rare. We become so self-involved that we fail to encourage others. We should all work to be encouraging because it is powerful. Simply share with others the ways you see God working in your heart and ways He has answered your prayers or has been providing for your needs. By sharing our daily devotional readings it helps others to want to read God's word more carefully and be more expectant of God opening his Word in new ways.

It is important for us to encourage other believers. The more we practice encouragement, the more natural this will become for us, and the more we will be able to strengthen each other.

"And let us consider how to stir up one another to love and good works, not neglecting to meet together, as is the habit of some, but encouraging one another, and all the more as you see the Day drawing near." **Hebrews 10: 24-25**

May you have a day of worship filled with encouragement.

Thirsty Soul

I woke up to another Lord's Day, and I am grateful. With Autumn soon to be upon us, I peeked outside to see the remaining blooms on the flowers, and the lawns were still green. God has blessed us with just enough rain this summer so we can enjoy the beauty of Summer's bounty. But, very soon, the flowers and gardens will turn to seed. This made me think of my own Soul. As long as I keep it watered with Scripture, worship, and prayer time, Jesus fills my soul with His beauty through each season of my life. If I find myself too busy for Jesus, my soul can turn brown and empty like a summer with too much heat and little rain. In many ways, our souls are like gardens that need regular watering to stay healthy. Spiritual watering involves reading the Bible, prayer and worshipping.

"As the deer pants for streams of water, ... so my soul pants for you, my God. Psalm 63:1 O God, you are my God, earnestly I seek you; my soul thirsts for you......" **Psalm 42:1**

Wishing you a day of worship that waters your soul and fills you with joy.

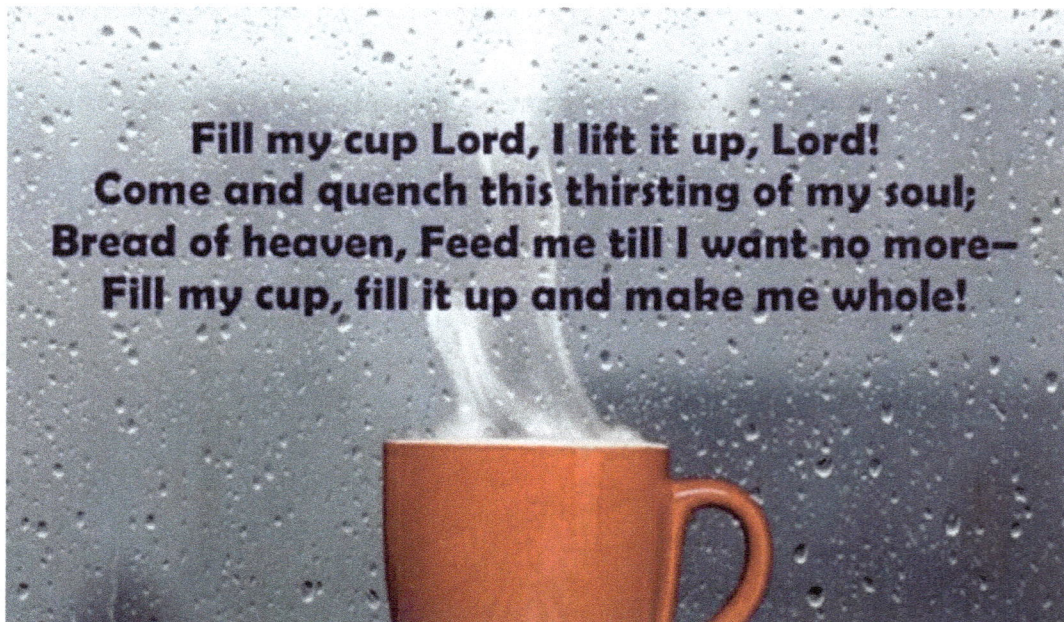

Fill my cup Lord, I lift it up, Lord!
Come and quench this thirsting of my soul;
Bread of heaven, Feed me till I want no more—
Fill my cup, fill it up and make me whole!

Choices

As I prepare for worship today, I am thinking about the power of choice. The choices I make either move me closer to God or farther away. I make choices all day long. Some of my choices are for small things, and some come with great responsibility. But every choice comes with a consequence that is either good or bad. I try to choose wisely, but like everyone, I make mistakes. When I make a bad choice, it is always because I did not pray about it first. One choice, through prayer, brings Jesus into the situation, and a bad choice brings Satan to work. One way releases light, and the other brings sin.

"May we abide in the commandments of Jesus when making decisions, seeking first the kingdom of God, and putting Him first in all things." **Proverbs 3:5-6**

"The mind of man plans his way, but the Lord directs his steps." **Proverbs 16:9**

I wish you a day of worship filled with the blessings of good choices through prayer.

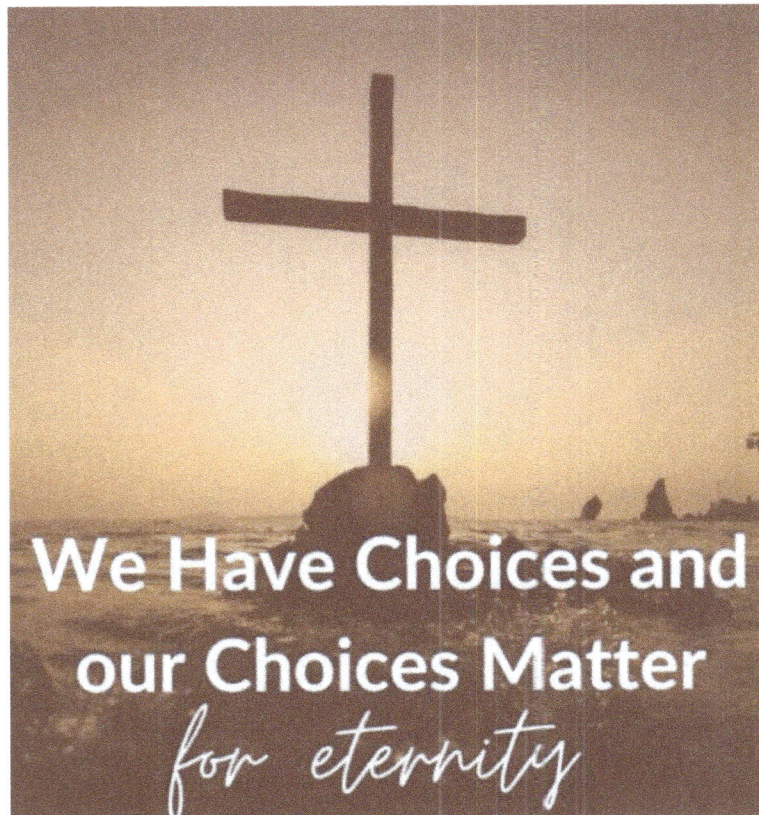

Holiday
Devotions

A NEW YEAR—A NEW DAY

As I prepare for worship this morning, I am thinking about the coming New Year. I have thoughts about the New Year that I would like to share with you.

God wants us to walk into the New Year with obedience. He asks us to be obedient, not because He wants to take from us. God doesn't want to take away; rather, He "wants to give us life and give it to us abundantly" this should apply to every day of the year.

We should get on our knees and ask Him for His blessings and then stand on our feet and do what God has asked us to do.

"He sees what's ahead and knows what's best for us." **John 10:10**

I wish you a joyful worship today that is filled with blessings.

Every day has
a new beginning,
a new blessing,
and a new hope.

The Joy of Sight and Sound

God has granted me another Lord's Day, and I am grateful. As I prepare for worship this morning, I am sitting in my family room listening to *Silent Night* and enjoying the beauty of our Christmas tree.

I have been so blessed to have the gifts of sight and sound, and the older I get, the more I appreciate them. With sight, I choose to see the beauty God has created for me to see. I am able to read scripture and see the faces of my loved ones. With hearing, God has gifted me with the sound of music and the sweet voices of my loved ones.

God has given me free will to choose how I use the gifts. I do not take these gifts for granted. God has given me the ability to both see and hear, and I should use these senses wisely. There is no better way to thank God for your sight than by giving a helping hand to someone in the dark or communicating with someone who can not hear.

"The hearing ear and the seeing eye, the Lord has made them both." **Proverbs 20:22**

As you worship today, I wish you the joy of the sight and sound of this Holy Christmas Season and a day filled with blessings.

The Gift

As I prepare for worship today, I can hardly believe Christmas is just a few days away. I am thinking about seeing so many ads and commercials about finding that special gift for giving. I wish the talk would be about the one true gift, the greatest gift, that has already been given and is freely given to all who want it.

That is the Gift of Salvation, and the Gift of Salvation is associated with Christmas because that is where it all began. Christmas is when God gave the greatest gift, the gift that no one can afford, no one can earn, and no one but God can give.

This gift is the gift of God's son, Jesus, and it is the responsibility of those of us who have received this gift to share it with those who are looking for it or do not know about it. Please share this gift with someone this Christmas Season, and let's keep Christ in Christmas.

"For God so loved the world, that he gave his only begotten Son, that whosoever believeth in him should not perish, but have everlasting life" **John 3:16**

Wishing each of you a joyful day of worship filled with blessings.

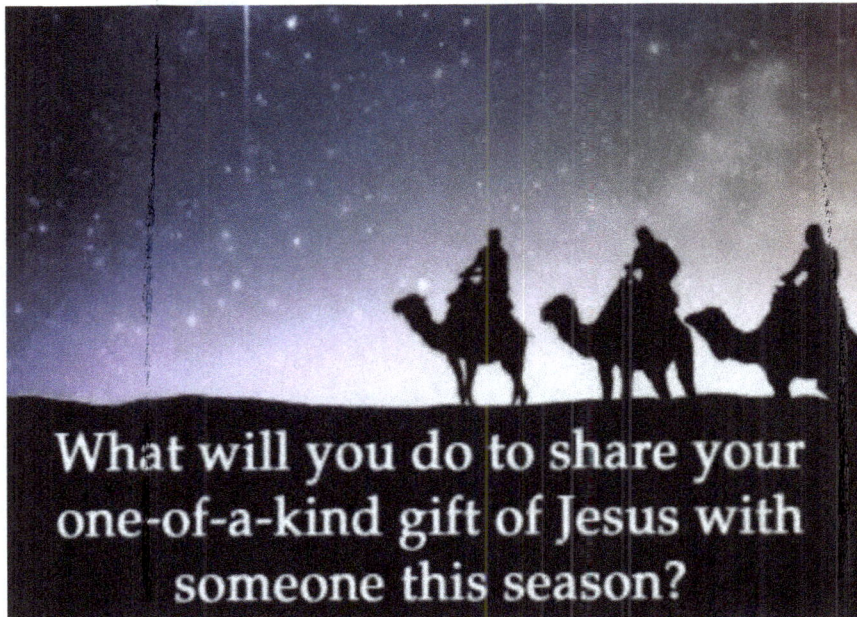

What will you do to share your one-of-a-kind gift of Jesus with someone this season?

Never Ending Christmas

As I prepare for worship on this Lord's Day, this Christmas Season surrounds me with beauty and joy. My Christmas tree lights are on, my Nativity scene is placed with care, and the fireplace mantle is covered in winter greenery. After the decorations have been packed away for next year, I know that the joy is not over.

I can have a never-ending Christmas celebration all year, sharing Jesus' love with all those around me. When I worship and give my best to Jesus, the joy continues all year long. The good news about Christmas is that even when the world or our circumstances change, the message of Christmas is timeless because it is about how Jesus came to give us love, hope and joy.

"She will give birth to a son, and you are to give him the name Jesus because he will save his people from their sins." **Matthew 1:21**

As you worship today, I wish you the joy of a never-ending Christmas and all the blessings that come with it.

Easter

God has granted me the most glorious Lord's Day to worship. Today is Easter, the Holiest of all days! This marks the Resurrection of Jesus three days after his death from crucifixion. Easter is the most important holiday for Christians. The resurrection is the foundation of the Christian belief. The resurrection gives Christians hope that there is life after this one. It demonstrates that God accepted Jesus' sacrifice on our behalf. It shows us that God has the power to raise us from the dead; in fact, it guarantees that!

> *"And if the Spirit of him who raised Jesus from the dead is living in you, he who raised Christ from the dead will also give life to your mortal."* **Romans 8:12**

> *"Blessed Be the God and Father of our Lord Jesus Chris! According to his great mercy, he has caused us to be born again to a living hope through the resurrection of Jesus Christ from the dead, to an inheritance that is imperishable, undefiled, and unfading, kept in Heaven for you."* **1 Peter 1: 3-4**

One of the most beloved hymns, *"Because He Lives,"* is sung *on* Easter in churches everywhere. As you worship today, I wish you the most Blessed Easter.

God's Love

Since I observed Ash Wednesday this past week, and this is the first Lord's Day of this Holy Season, I have much to think about. This Holy Season is so full of hope and promise. I have great hope and faith through scripture and prayer, especially during this time. I would not like to think about where I would be if Jesus had not sacrificed his life for me. I have come to know that there is no greater love than God's love for me. God's love is faithful and merciful. The faithful love of the Lord never ends. His mercies never cease. Great is His faithfulness. God's love is compassionate.

> *"So we have come to know and to believe the love that God has for us. God is love, and whoever abides in love abides in God, and God abides in him."* **1 John 4:16**
>
> *"God's love is everlasting and loving-kindness."* **Jeremiah 31:3**

It is time to be preparing our hearts for the Cross, the Tomb, and The Resurrection. Wherever you worship today, I wish you God's love and a day filled with blessings.

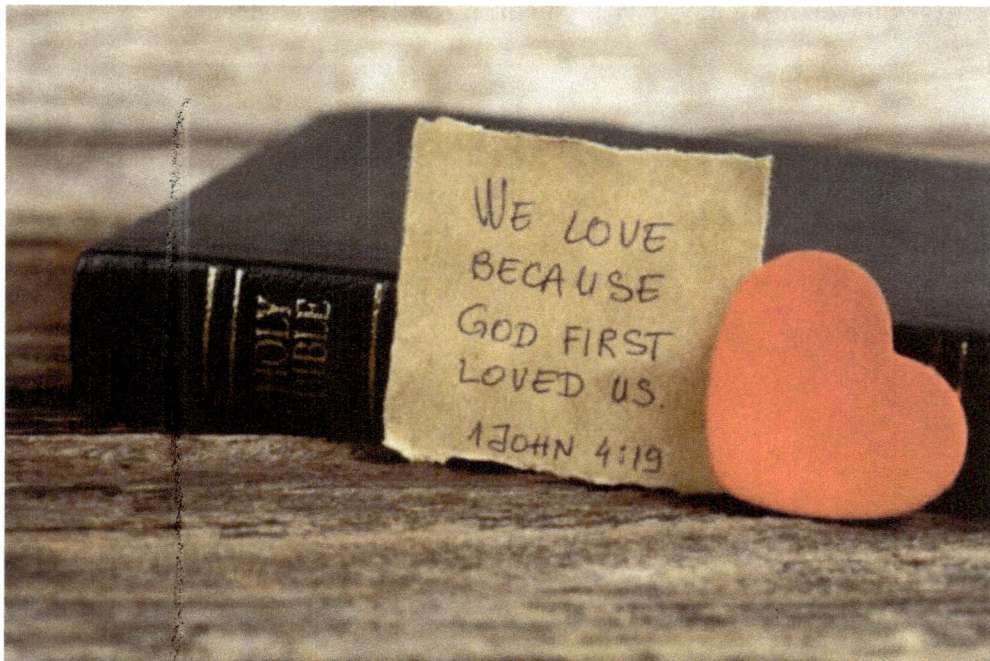

Holy Week

As I prepare for worship today, my mind is on this coming of Holy Week and what it means. Maundy Thursday is when Jesus washed his disciple's feet to show them humility. It is also the night of the Last Supper, where the teaching of Holy Communion takes place. It is also the time when Jesus was betrayed by Judas.

Good Friday is when Jesus was crucified and took all our sins upon himself. Then, His body was placed in a tomb.

Easter Sunday is the Resurrection of Jesus.

"And as they were eating, he took bread, and after blessing it, broke it up and gave it to them, and said "take; this is my body." And he took a cup, and he said to them, "this is my blood of the covenants which is poured out for" **Mark 14:22-24**

"When he received the drink, Jesus said, "It is finished. "With that, he bowed his head and gave up his spirit." **John 19:30**

"Christ Jesus who died-more than that, who was raised to life-is at the right hand of God and is also interceding for us." **Romans 8:34**

I wish you a beautiful day of worship and prepare your heart for Holy Week.

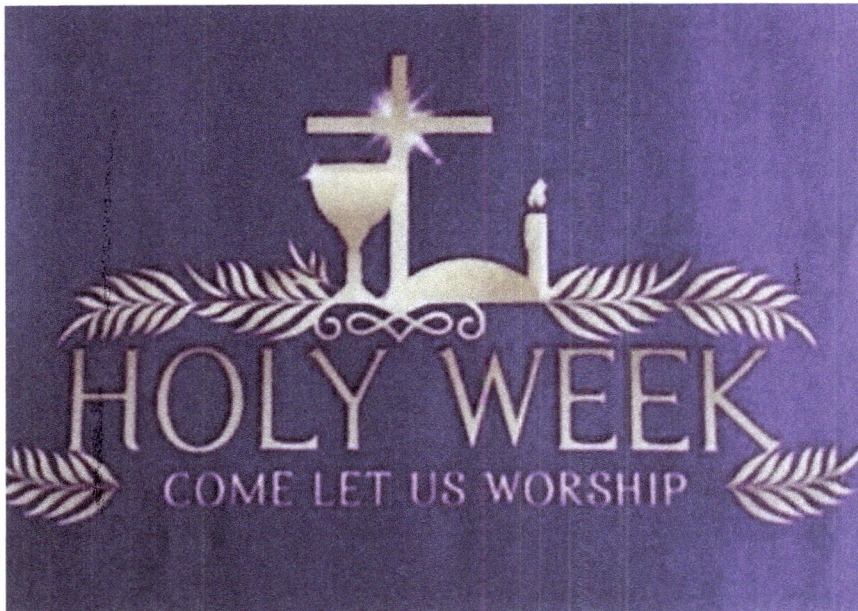

Palm Sunday

Palm Sunday is the beginning of Holy Week. Palm Sunday is the day Jesus rode a donkey into Jerusalem to celebrate Passover. The crowds of people waved palms and laid their cloaks before him to honor him. This also fulfilled many prophecies in the Old Testament, including Isaiah and Zechariah.

As I prepare myself for Easter, I feel mixed emotions. I feel sorrow that my sins nailed Jesus to the cross, and I also am grateful that Jesus paid for my pardon.

"So they took the branches of the palm trees and went out to meet him, crying out Hosanna! Blessed is he who comes in the name of the Lord, even the King of Israel." **John 12:13**

As the words in one of my favorite hymns say,

Jesus paid it all. I hear the savior say; thy strength indeed is small Child of weakness, watch and pray, find in me thine all in all, 'Cause Jesus paid it all. All to him, I owe. Sin had left a crimson stain; he washed it white as snow.

Please join me each day of this coming week in prayer for what God gave us on this week many years ago. Wishing you a day of meaningful worship as you reflect on this Palm Sunday.

The Old Rugged Cross

As I prepare for worship today, my mind is on this Holy Season and the Cross. Life is wasted if we do not grasp the glory of the Cross, cherish it for the treasure that it is, and cling to it as the greatest gift ever given to us. The cross is the center of God's plan of salvation. The cross is the main symbol of Christianity. For me, the cross means redemption and sacrifice and triumph over sin and also death.

Paul tells us this:

"May I never boast except in the cross of our Lord Jesus Christ through which the world has been crucified to me, and I to the world." **Galatians 6: 14**

One of my favorite hymns is *"The Old Rugged Cross."* The lyrics speak to my heart. I find myself singing the chorus often:

> *"So I'll cherish the old rugged cross,*
> *Till my trophies, at last, I lay down;*
> *I will cling to the old rugged cross,*
> *And exchange it someday for a crown."*

Wishing you a blessed of worship and preparing your heart for this Holy Season

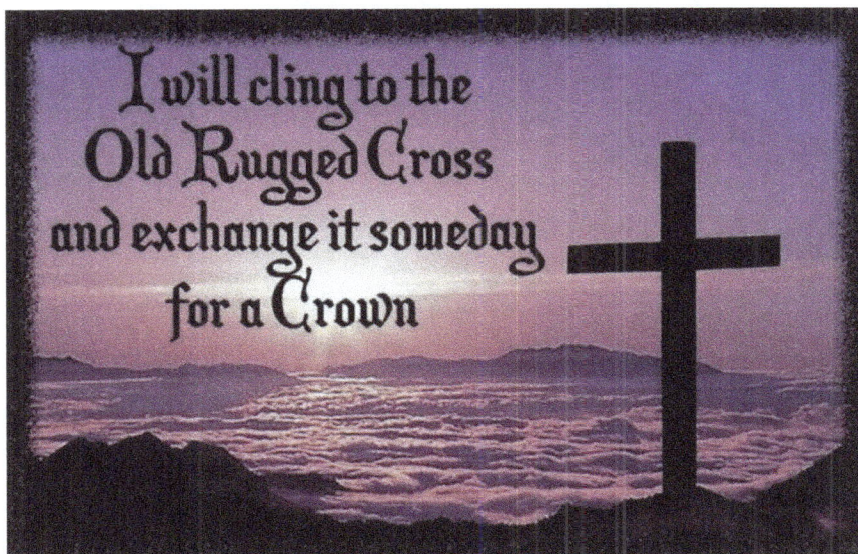

Veterans

On this Lord's Day, as I lay all toasty and warm in my bed before getting up to prepare for worship, I am thinking about our Veterans of my time. I see in my mind a WWll Vet freezing in a fox hole, a Korean Vet charging up a hill, a Vietnam Vet in a wet bug-infested jungle and all of them fighting for their lives and their country. I see many young people with families now who fought in the sands of Iraq, the Middle East, and Afghanistan.

One of my most heartfelt prayers today is that we all get up from our warm and comfortable beds and devote time to worship and thank our Savior for all the Vets for what they had to do for me and you so we are able to worship openly and live our lives in freedom. At the very least, we owe them that because the wars do not end for them when they come home. I was reminded of this scripture this morning.

"For the LORD, your God is the one who goes with you to fight for you against your enemies to give you victory." **Deuteronomy 20:4**

Wishing each of you a day filled with blessings and thankfulness.

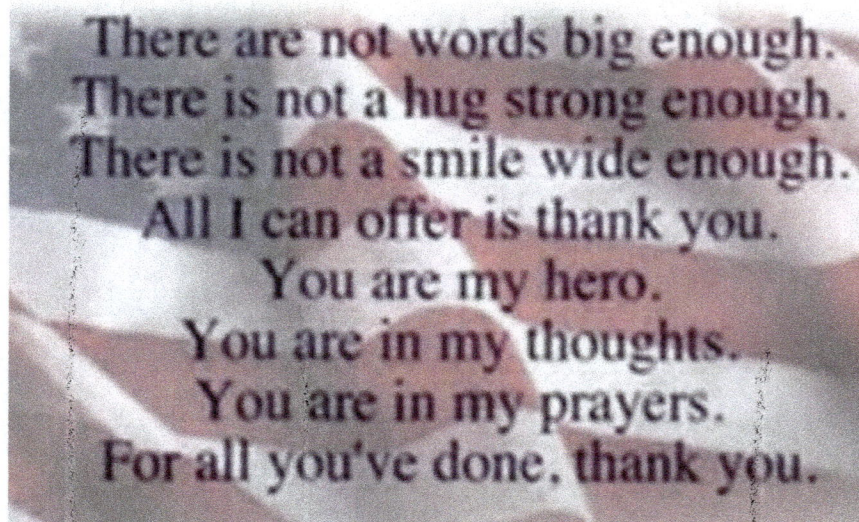

There are not words big enough.
There is not a hug strong enough.
There is not a smile wide enough.
All I can offer is thank you.
You are my hero.
You are in my thoughts.
You are in my prayers.
For all you've done, thank you.

Thanks and Giving

As I prepare for worship on this special Lord's Day before Thanksgiving, my mind is filled with how blessed I have been my whole life. Just like everyone, there have been some very hard times, but God has always walked me through them with His grace and mercy. He has never abandoned me. This Thanksgiving, as I grow older and look back on my life, I realize there have been blessings that I did not recognize at the time they were given to me. I am still growing in my spiritual life, and I hope each of you is, too.

When we give thanks in the truest sense of the biblical word, we offer God our praises and acknowledge to Him that He is the Giver of all good gifts.

"Therefore, since we are receiving a kingdom that can not be shaken, let us be thankful, and so worship God acceptably with reverence and awe," for our God is a consuming fire."
Hebrews 12:28

"Giving thanks always and for everything to God the Father in the name of our Lord Jesus Christ."
Ephesians 5:20

Wishing each of you a day of worship filled with thankfulness and blessings.

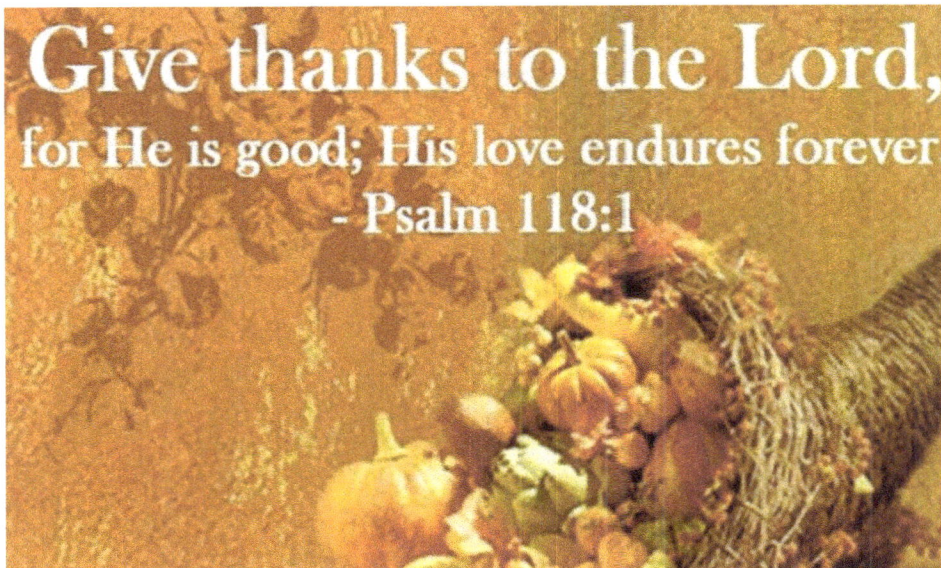

Give thanks to the Lord, for He is good; His love endures forever - Psalm 118:1

Thanksgiving

Preparing for worship on this Lord's Day, my thoughts are on Thanksgiving. In today's world, it can become easy to forget at times how dependent I am on God for everything, even the air I breathe. I am reminded today to ask God to open my eyes to all the blessings He has bestowed on me and give me a fresh spirit of gratitude and thankfulness. Not just during this season of the year but always.

I pray that I am always reminded of just how blessed I am and that I never forget to show my thankfulness in prayer, acts of kindness and worship.

"It is good to give thanks to the Lord." **Psalms 92:1**

Wishing you a day blessed with a grateful heart as you worship our Lord with praise.

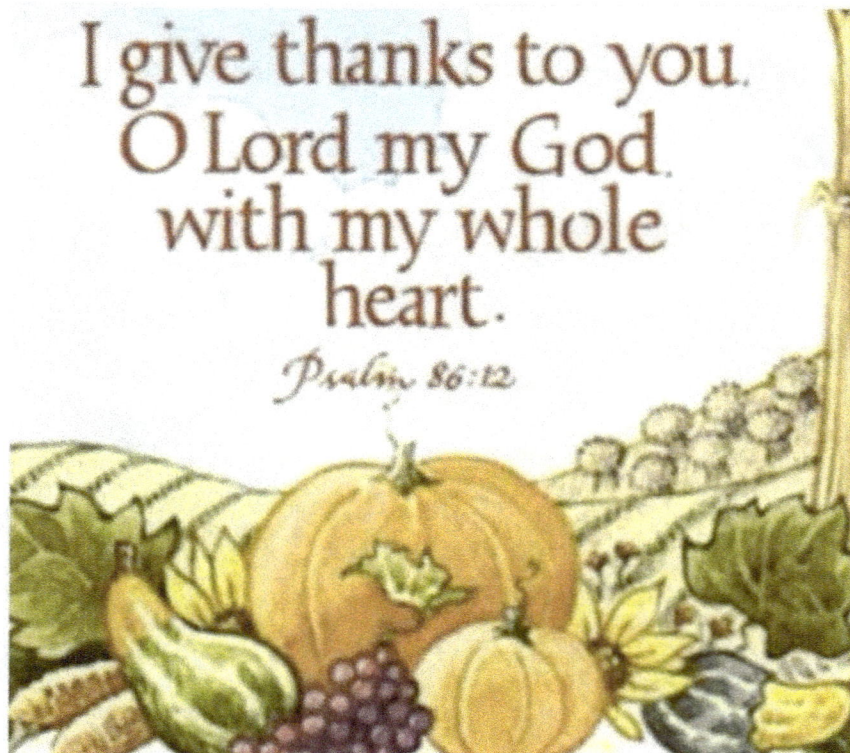

I give thanks to you. O Lord my God. with my whole heart. Psalm 86:12

Fourth of July

As I prepare for worship this morning, I do so with a grateful heart. We are preparing to celebrate the birth of our Great Nation. Our freedom has been won through sacrifice. Sacrifice is a God-given value, and God's word brings meaning honor to the sacrifices of His Son and our soldiers. I am free to praise God where and when I want to every day, but the Sabbath is the most special day to worship.

With all the turmoil in this world today, I worry that our next generations may not have the freedom to worship openly. I pray that God will/ continue to shine his favor on us. And that we will once again become One Nation under God.

> *"Blessed is the Nation whose God is the Lord, the people He has chosen as His heritage."* **Psalm 33:12**

> *"Now the Lord is the Spirit, and where the Spirit of the Lord is, there is freedom."* **2 Corinthians 3:17**

I pray that we each make time to worship today and teach our children what a gift it is to do so. Hope everyone has a blessed day.

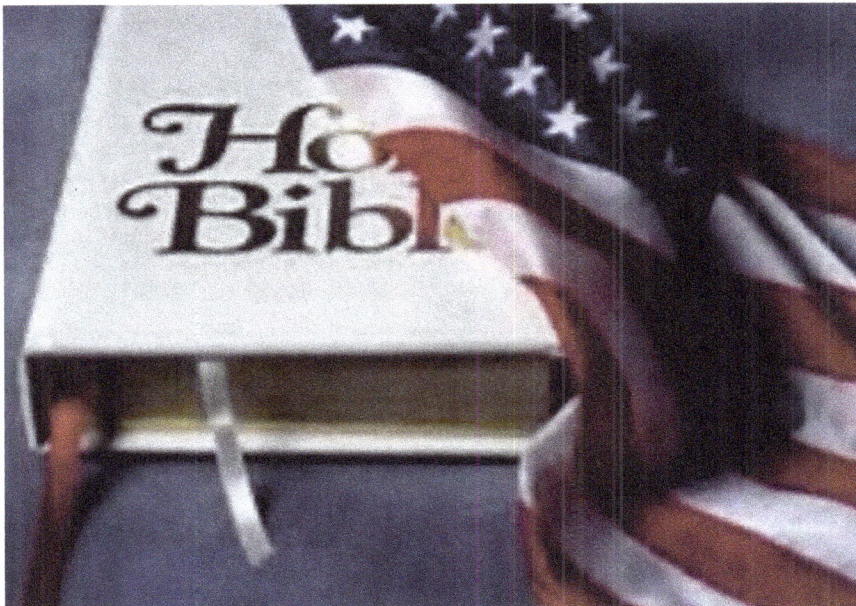

Celebrate Freedom

As I prepare for worship today, I am thinking about freedom as the 4th of July and how blessed we are that we live in this Country of freedom. This freedom was bought for us with many kinds of sacrifices, and I am grateful. But now, I am thinking about the greatest kind of freedom. The Fourth of July is an awesome time to remind yourself of our freedom in Christ and what that means for living a life that honors God. The kind of freedom that can only come from seeking to understand and obey God's Word. True freedom comes from knowing the truth about who we are, who God is, and what He has done for us. Freedom is not an excuse to sin; instead it's a responsibility that should be used to serve others.

"Now the Lord is the Spirit, and where the Spirit of the Lord is, there is freedom." **2 Corinthians 3:17**

Let us all celebrate the greatest freedom that Jesus gave us from His sacrifice on the cross, along with the blessing of the freedom we celebrate within our Country.

Wishing everyone a day of worship, celebrating our freedom in Christ.

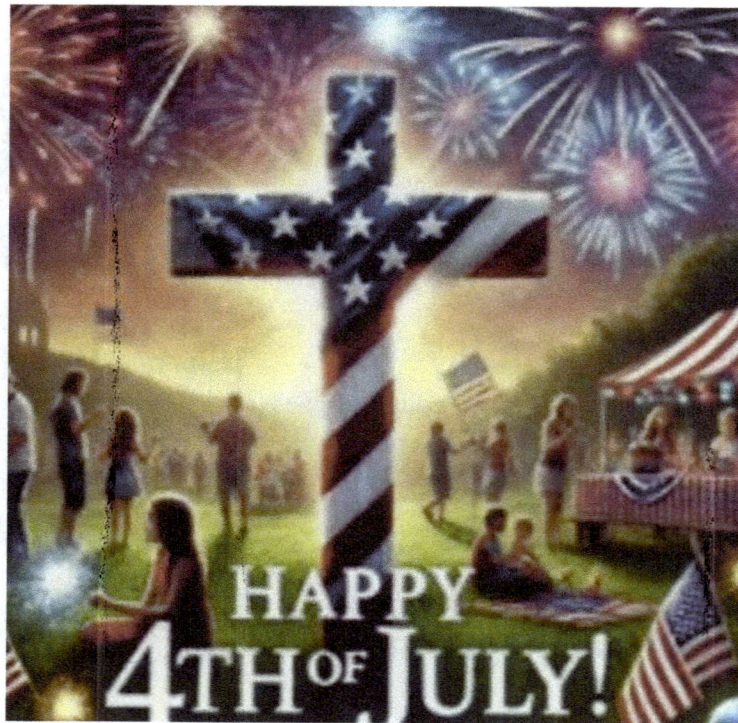

Happy Mother's Day

On this Lord's Day, as we worship, we are also celebrating Mother's Day. My Mom is now in Heaven, and I have that blessed assurance. I would love to go back in time to when I was a small child for just one worship service to be snuggled in the pew with my Mom. I loved her sweet fragrance and the comfort of her arm wrapped around my shoulders. I remember her smile as I showed her what I made in Sunday School that morning and how it would bring such joy to me. On Mother's Day, she always wore a beautiful fresh corsage that Dad gave her.

These remembrances are blessings that I will always hold dear, and I thank God for them.

"Her children arise up and call her blessed; her husband also, and he praiseth her." **Proverbs 31:28**

"Honor her for that her hands have done" **Proverbs 31:31**

I wish you a very special day of worship filled with blessing and honor Mothers.

Father's Day

On this very special Lord's Day, we are celebrating and honoring our fathers. I am worshipping today with a thankful and grateful heart because God gifted me with a Christian Dad who taught me about God's love through his actions and his love for Jesus. Then, I was blessed with a Christian husband who loved me and his children unconditionally. Becoming a father is an opportunity to love and care for children as God loves and cares for us. The task of leading a family requires bravery, decisiveness and devotion to God.

"Fathers do not provoke your children, lest they become discouraged." **Colossians 3:21**

"As a father shows compassion to his children, so the Lord shows compassion to those who fear him." **Psalms 103:13**

My hope today is that everyone, in some way, is blessed with a Christian man in their life, but most importantly, that everyone comes to know our Father who art in Heaven.

Wishing you a very blessed day as we honor our Fathers.

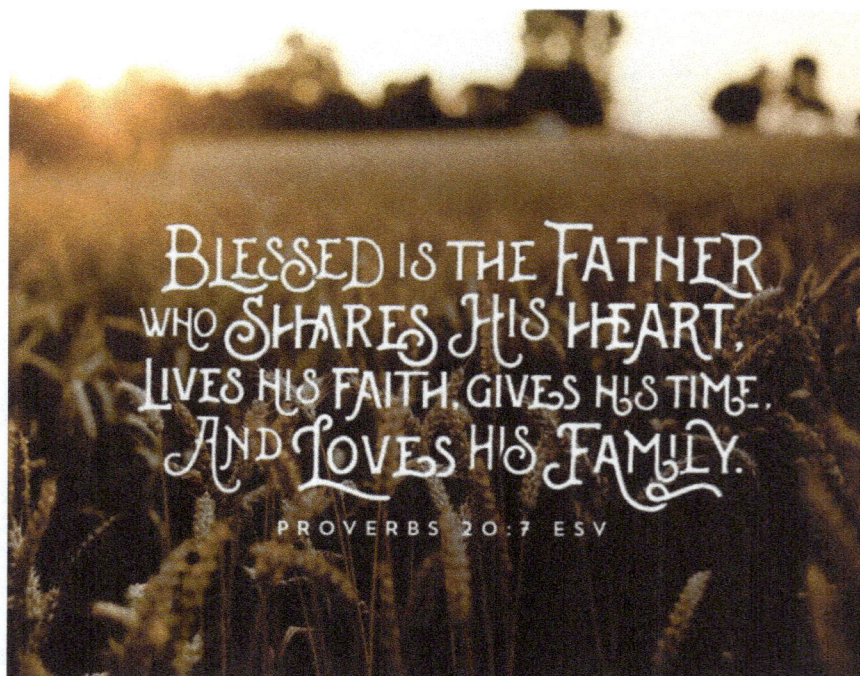

BLESSED IS THE FATHER WHO SHARES HIS HEART, LIVES HIS FAITH, GIVES HIS TIME, AND LOVES HIS FAMILY.

PROVERBS 20:7 ESV

"Don't worry about anything; instead, pray about everything. Tell God what you need, and thank him for all he has done." **Philippians 4:6**

Prayer List

_____

_____

_____

_____

_____

_____

_____

_____

_____

_____

_____

_____

_____

_____

_____

_____

_____

_____

_____

_____

_____

_____